microwave speed meals

microwave cooking library®

by barbara methven

microwave cooking library®

Just how fast is fast? *Microwave Speed Meals* challenges all previous standards for fast meals. Can you actually make a light meal in 10 minutes? Of course! And that's the maximum time for most foods in the Quick Bite section. More substantial meals take longer (about ½ hour), but even the gourmet dinner parties clock in at record time.

Timesaving tips and speed cooking shortcuts help you streamline your kitchen technique. You'll also find ideas for shopping, storage and kitchen utensils designed to shave precious minutes off the total time you spend preparing and serving meals.

Best of all, you'll discover that cutting the time you spend in the kitchen does not mean cutting quality. Speed meals satisfy both the need for good nutrition and appetizing taste. The microwave oven changed the way you cook. *Microwave Speed Meals* will change the way you microwave.

Barbara Methven

CREDITS:
Design & Production: Cy DeCosse Incorporated
Art Director: Delores Swanson
Project Director: Peggy Ramette
Project Managers: Lisa Bergerud, Deborah Bialik, Rachel Imbrock
Home Economists: Sue Brue, Bonnie Ellingboe, Peggy Ramette, Ann Stuart, Grace Wells
Dietitian: Patricia D. Godfrey, R.D.
Consultants: Sue Brue, Bonnie Ellingboe, Gloria Kirchman, Grace Wells
Editors: Janice Cauley, Bernice Maehren
Director of Development Planning & Production: Jim Bindas
Production Manager: Amelia Merz
Production Art Supervisor: Julie Churchill
Typesetting: Kevin D. Frakes, Linda Schloegel
Production Staff: Joe Fahey, Melissa Grabanski, Jim Huntley, Mark Jacobson, Duane John, Yelena Konrardy, Daniel Meyers, Greg Wallace, Nik Wogstad
Studio Manager: Rebecca DaWald
Photographers: Rex Irmen, John Lauenstein, Bill Lindner, Mark Macemon, Mette Nielsen, Mike Parker, Cathleen Shannon
Food Stylists: Sue Brue, Bobbette Destiche
Color Separations: Scantrans
Printing: R. R. Donnelley & Sons (0191)

Additional volumes in the Microwave Cooking Library series are available from the publisher:

- Basic Microwaving
- Recipe Conversion for Microwave
- Microwaving Meats
- Microwave Baking & Desserts
- Microwaving Meals in 30 Minutes
- Microwaving on a Diet
- Microwaving Fruits & Vegetables
- Microwaving Convenience Foods
- Microwaving for Holidays & Parties
- Microwaving for One & Two
- The Microwave & Freezer
- 101 Microwaving Secrets
- Microwaving Light & Healthy
- Microwaving Poultry & Seafood
- Microwaving America's Favorites
- Microwaving Fast & Easy Main Dishes
- More Microwaving Secrets
- Microwaving Light Meals & Snacks
- Holiday Microwave Ideas
- Easy Microwave Menus
- Low-fat Microwave Meals
- Cool Quick Summer Microwaving
- Ground Beef Microwave Meals

CY DE COSSE INCORPORATED
Chairman: Cy DeCosse
President: James B. Maus
Executive Vice President: William B. Jones

Library of Congress Cataloging-in-Publication Data

Methven, Barbara.
  Microwave speed meals / by Barbara Methven.

  p. cm. — (Microwave cooking library)

  ISBN 0-86573-570-0 (hardcover)
  1. Microwave cookery   I. Title.   II. Series.
TX832.M3964   1990
641.5'882 — dc20   90-46447
                                                          CIP

Contents

What You Need to Know Before You Start

Much of the time consumed by food preparation is spent before you ever start to cook. Reducing that total time will help you get the most speed from these easy-to-assemble, quick-cooking recipes.

The Organized Kitchen

A little time spent getting organized will streamline your kitchen so you can accomplish more in less time. Don't waste time hunting for things. Organize your food-storage areas so you can find ingredients quickly and know at a glance if supplies need replenishing.

Store cooking equipment you use frequently in the most convenient and accessible spots, where you can find it fast. Tuck rarely used items away in a corner or on a top shelf. Group small utensils according to use so you can quickly select the one you need. Once you have found the right places for these items, make sure they are returned there after every use.

Planning Ahead

Keep a pad of paper handy in your kitchen so you can jot down the staples you need to replace. Plan meals for several days or a week in advance. Once you have chosen the recipes, list all ingredients you will need to buy. If you are following the menu suggestions that accompany each main dish, include those foods on your list. Before you shop, revise the list, grouping items that are found together, like fresh produce, meats or frozen foods.

Speed Shopping

To reduce time spent in travel between home and store or waiting in the check-out line, shop once a week at a time when the market is not busy. It is fun to explore a new supermarket, but when you are in a hurry, shop in a familiar store. You will not waste precious time searching the aisles for pasta, condiments or household products.

When you bring foods home, take the time to put them away in the proper places in your speed-storage areas. If you have a little more time, prepare some ingredients for the week ahead. You might wash and dry lettuce or chop and freeze onion and green pepper.

Cooking in a Hurry

When you're cooking in a hurry, organization pays. First read through the entire recipe, so there will be no surprises later on. Assemble the ingredients; check the emergency substitution chart (page 9), if necessary. Get out cooking and serving utensils. If you've organized your food and equipment storage, you'll find everything fast.

Start any food that has a longer cooking time, like conventionally cooked pasta or rice. You can measure and mix ingredients for microwaved foods while the water comes to a boil. If all foods in the meal are quick-cooking, measure all the ingredients *before* you start to cook.

While food microwaves, set the table. A basket already stocked with silverware, napkins, salt and pepper simplifies table setting and saves steps.

More Money Than Time

Many supermarkets offer ready-made foods, as well as ready-to-cook ingredients with tedious or time-consuming preparations already done. When saving time means more than saving money, make use of these specialties:

Produce: cleaned and cut-up vegetables; washed spinach; preshredded cabbage; lettuce mixtures; cut-up melons and pineapple.

Dairy: preshredded and pre-sliced cheese.

Meats: fresh, boneless, skinned chicken breasts; fresh turkey breast slices and tenderloins; precooked, boneless chicken or turkey.

Deli: fully cooked sliced beef, ham, turkey and chicken; deli salads; deli side dishes; deli desserts.

Frozen foods: snipped chives; chopped onion or bell pepper.

Bakery: rolls; biscuits; corn bread.

Miscellaneous: microwave pasta; quick-cooking rice and couscous; prepared bread crumbs and croutons; tomato paste in tubes.

How to Use This Book

Apple-Cinnamon Pork Chops

4 pork loin chops (5 to 6 oz. each), about 3/4 inch thick
1 large apple, cut into 1/4-inch slices
1/4 cup raisins
1 tablespoon cornstarch
1 tablespoon packed brown sugar
1/4 teaspoon salt
1/4 teaspoon ground cinnamon
1/2 cup apple juice

Arrange pork chops in 8-inch square baking dish. Arrange apple slices evenly over chops. Sprinkle with raisins.

In small mixing bowl, combine remaining ingredients. Pour over pork chops. Cover with wax paper or microwave cooking paper. Microwave at 70% (Medium High) for 14 to 18 minutes, or until pork is tender and no longer pink near bone, stirring sauce mixture once. Let stand, covered, for 5 minutes.

Per Serving: Calories: 364 • Protein: 32 g. • Carbohydrate: 22 g. • Fat: 16 g. • Cholesterol: 89 mg. • Sodium: 189 mg.
Exchanges: 4½ lean meat, 1½ fruit, ½ fat

4 servings

Apple Cinnamon Pork Chops
Mixed Vegetables   Cloverleaf Rolls

61

Get ready to break your previous record for speedy meal preparation. Even with a microwave oven, cooking has never been this fast. The recipes in *Microwave Speed Meals* take advantage of every short-cut available to get you out of the kitchen and to get a meal on the table in record time. Per serving nutritional values follow each recipe. When a recipe serves 4 to 6 persons, the analysis applies to the greater number of servings. In the case of alternate ingredients, the analysis refers to the first ingredient listed.

Quick Bites. Depending upon how hungry you are, Quick Bites make either a light meal or a hearty snack. None of the recipes call for more than eight ingredients; many require less. The longest cooking times are about ten minutes; some recipes microwave in as little as one minute.

Each Quick Bite category presents a simple idea and gives you seven to twelve different ways to use it. With this much variety, you could serve a different Quick Bite every day for a month and still have more recipes to try.

Super-quick Meals. The super-quick main dishes call for no more than ten ingredients and can be ready in thirty minutes or less. For maximum speed, they use fresh meats that cook quickly, precooked deli meats, canned meats, even leftovers. Menu suggestions that complete the meal and keep preparation time within the thirty-minute time limit are given.

Super-quick Side Dishes. These fast dishes complete your meal in short order. To maximize speed, they use frozen or canned vegetables, instant rice and other easily available products you keep in your speed pantry.

Speedy Gourmet. For easy entertaining, most of these meals can be ready in less than an hour. Each menu includes two or three recipes, each of which uses no more than twelve ingredients. Asterisks mark menu suggestions that complete the meal.

Fast Finishes. Create these appealing desserts with minimum time, effort and ingredients. A few are made ahead and refrigerated or frozen.

7

Speed Food Storage

The secret of speed food storage is order. Where space is limited, you may need to be selective in what you keep on hand and conscientious about replacing items as they are used. Ample storage space allows you to stock back-up items, but demands well-planned organization.

Even more important than having an efficient storage plan is sticking with it. If you shove a new supply of canned goods in at the front of your pantry, you will have to hunt through the disorder later, and you may lose track of some items.

Pantry and Refrigerator Tips

Package size determines the location of some items. In general, in the pantry, group similar products, such as canned meats and fish, or rice, couscous and pasta. In the refrigerator, keep opened jars of pickles, olives and relish together, store fruits and vegetables in separate crispers.

If you use a deep cupboard as pantry space, store frequently used items toward the front. Tape a diagram or inventory to the door so you will know what is hidden at the back.

Freezer Hints

More than in any other food storage area, organization is necessary in the freezer. Storage life of many frozen foods, especially meats, is limited — about 6 months in an upright or chest freezer or 1 month in the freezer compartment of a refrigerator. Quality deteriorates after that, so it is important to know what you have, how long you have had it and where it is. Take the time to label and date frozen foods, using a waterproof marker and masking or freezer tape. Group similar foods, then check routinely for outdated or forgotten items.

Stocking Up

The Speed Food Storage list (opposite) suggests foods you may want to keep on hand. In addition to products used in the recipes and menus for speed meals, it includes basics like flour, sugar and condiments, plus useful "emergency supplies" like canned chicken and frozen hamburger. On those occasions when you are ready to cook but lack an ingredient, consult the Substitution Chart (opposite).

Speed Food Storage

Canned and Bottled Foods:

Fruits: mandarin orange segments, pineapple chunks, cherry and apple pie fillings

Vegetables: corn, sliced mushrooms

Tomatoes: juice, plum, whole, stewed, paste, sauce, spaghetti sauce

Beans: garbanzo, Great Northern, black, kidney, refried

Meats: chunk chicken and ham

Fish and seafood: clams, crab, salmon, shrimp, tuna

Broth: beef and chicken

Oil: olive and vegetable

Vinegar: white, cider, wine, fruit, herb

Seasoning sauces: hot pepper, soy, Worcestershire

Other: condensed soups, bamboo shoots, green chilies, pimiento, water chestnuts

Dry Products:

Bread: unseasoned and seasoned dry bread crumbs, cornflake crumbs, croutons, stuffing mix

Grains: long-grain and instant rice, bulgur

Pasta: cappellini, vermicelli, spaghetti, fettucini, orzo, couscous

Mixes: soup, gravy and sauce, pudding, buttermilk baking mix

Staples: constarch, cornmeal, all-purpose flour, rolled oats, brown sugar, sugar

Seasoning: salt, pepper, herbs, spices, seasoning blends

Other: raisins, shredded coconut

Refrigerated:

Meats: bacon, ground beef, chicken breasts or fish fillets

Fruits: peaches, melons, raspberries, blueberries, apples

Vegetables: carrots, celery, green and red peppers, salad greens, green onions

Fresh pasta: tortellini, ravioli, linguine, fettucini

Breads: tortillas, lefse, soft cracker bread, pita

Dairy: eggs, milk, margarine or butter, sour cream, yogurt, cream cheese

Condiments: catsup, chili and taco sauce, salsa, horseradish, mayonnaise or salad dressing, Dijon and prepared mustard, salad dressings, bottled lemon juice, jams and jellies, olives, pickles

Frozen:

Meats: ground beef and turkey, chicken breasts, turkey breast slices and tenderloins, fish fillets, shrimp, scallops

Fruits: blueberries, raspberries, strawberries, peaches

Vegetables: corn, peas and carrots, peas, broccoli cuts, crinkle-cut carrots, chopped green pepper and onion

Breads: French, tortillas, pita

Pasta: fresh tortellini, ravioli, fettucini, linguine

Other: shredded cheese, fruit juice concentrate, ice cream, frozen yogurt, sherbet

Substitution Chart

Ingredient:	Substitution:
1 lb. gound beef	1 lb. ground turkey
2 cups cut-up cooked chicken	2 cups cut-up cooked turkey, or 2 cans (5 oz. each) chunk chicken
2 cups cubed fully cooked ham	2 cups cubed fully cooked turkey ham
1 can tuna	1 can boneless, skinless salmon
1 cup chicken or beef broth	1 cup hot water plus 1 teaspoon instant chicken or beef bouillon granules
1 cup milk	½ cup evaporated milk plus ½ cup water
1 cup tomato sauce	6 tablespoons tomato paste plus ½ cup water
1 cup tomato juice	½ cup tomato sauce plus ½ cup water
1 cup catsup or chili sauce	1 can (8 oz.) tomato sauce plus ½ cup sugar and 2 tablespoons white vinegar
White wine	Equal amount of apple juice or cider
4 oz. uncooked fresh pasta	2 oz. uncooked dry cappellini or vermicelli
1 tablespoon cornstarch	2 tablespoons all-purpose flour
¼ cup unseasoned dry bread crumbs	1 slice crisp, dry bread, crushed
Fresh garlic clove	⅛ teaspoon garlic powder or ¼ teaspoon instant minced garlic
1 small onion or ¼ cup minced fresh onion	1 teaspoon onion powder or 1 tablespoon instant minced onion
1 medium onion	2 teaspoons onion powder or 2 tablespoons instant minced onion
1 medium lemon	2 to 3 tablespoons lemon juice
1 medium orange	¼ to ⅓ cup orange juice
Fresh snipped parsley	⅓ to ½ amount of dry parsley flakes
1 tablespoon snipped fresh herbs	1 teaspoon dried herbs, crushed
1 teaspoon Italian seasoning	¼ teaspoon each basil, marjoram, oregano and thyme leaves

Timesaving Devices

The right tool for the task, in good condition and in the right place, saves time when you are in a hurry. Well-sharpened knives speed food preparation; dull knives are dangerous as well as slow. A drawer divider keeps small utensils organized and at hand when needed.

Food Processor chops, slices or grates foods in quantity. Use it to prepare ingredients you can store in the refrigerator for use all week, such as chopped parsley, onion, green pepper and celery, or grated cheese.

Salad Spinner extracts most of the water from greens. Wash them ahead of time, spin, then wrap loosely in paper or cloth towels, place in a plastic bag and refrigerate.

Mandolines julienne or slice in a variety of thicknesses.

Tools that are indispensable for any well-equipped kitchen are a vegetable parer, a very sharp 12-inch chef's knife and a medium-size whisk.

Kitchen Shears snip herbs, divide poultry or pizza and cut up tomatoes right in the can.

Rolling mincer or mini-chopper chops small amounts quickly.

Gadgets speed special tasks. Shown clockwise from upper left are garlic press, jar opener, grater with built-in measure, bar bottle dispenser for drip-free pouring of oil and vinegar, gravy skimmer, citrus reamer, zester and egg slicer.

Timesaving Tips

A little advance planning or efficient use of a few spare moments saves time and effort at meal preparation time, when every moment counts.

Save time by paying attention to details. The cooking techniques that promote even heating also reduce microwaving time. Well-prepared food actually gets done faster than food that is carelessly prepared.

Cutting foods into uniform pieces allows them to microwave evenly. Smaller pieces cook faster than larger ones. To speed slicing of vegetables, place up to 3 vegetables side by side on cutting board.

Covering foods speeds cooking, retains moisture or prevents spattering (saving cleanup time).

Stirring foods promotes faster, more even microwaving. When foods cannot be stirred, rearrange pieces or reposition the dish in the oven.

Standing time may be used to heat another food, toss a salad or set the table.

Timesaving Tips (Continued)

Store canned broth in the refrigerator for fast and easy fat removal.

Place mozzarella cheese in the freezer for 15 minutes to make shredding easier.

Chop onion and green pepper when you have the time. Spread in a shallow pan to freeze, then break apart and store in freezer bags up to 1 month.

Keep a tube of tomato paste in the refrigerator for a subtle touch of flavor in sauces.

Process a bunch of washed and *thoroughly dried* parsley; refrigerate in covered container up to 1 week.

Refrigerate washed bouquets of parsley, cilantro or dill in glasses of water, covered with a plastic bag; they stay fresh up to 2 weeks.

Shred cheese with the food processor. Refrigerate in covered glass jars up to 1 week or freeze up to 1 month.

Quick Salads

For nutrition, fresh taste and speedy preparation, complement your main dish with a salad. Wash and tear up salad greens when you bring them home from the market. Dry thoroughly with a salad spinner, paper towels or a fresh dish towel. Wrap loosely in dry paper or cloth towels, place in a plastic bag and refrigerate. Well-dried greens stay crisp and fresh several days.

Toss salad greens with one to three of the following: cut-up raw vegetables, marinated artichoke hearts or mushrooms, avocado slices, alfalfa or bean sprouts, cooked crumbled bacon, shredded or cubed cheese, grated Parmesan cheese, chopped hard-cooked egg, olives, croutons, chow mein noodles, sunflower seeds, crushed melba toast.

Slice tomato, cucumber and onion to serve with your favorite dressing as a change from salad greens.

Add leftover cooked vegetables, potatoes or legumes to tossed salad, or bind them with seasoned mayonnaise and serve on bed of lettuce.

Scatter a handful of fresh raspberries, a few apple slices or canned mandarin oranges over lettuce or prewashed spinach and toss with vinaigrette.

Quick Vegetable Toppers

Provide flavor, color and texture contrast to vegetables with a quick topper. When time is short, rely on frozen or canned vegetables. For variety, try one of the frozen vegetable combinations.

Shredded cheese melts over hot-from-the-microwave potatoes, asparagus, broccoli or cauliflower.

Bacon, microwaved crisp and crumbled, complements many vegetables. A few are: carrots, artichokes, beans, celery, pearl onions, peas, potatoes, mashed squash, spinach and zucchini.

Shredded Parmesan cheese imparts an Italian character to zucchini, asparagus, beans or broccoli. Mix with snipped fresh herbs or toasted crumbs, if desired.

Chopped chives garnish any vegetable. For more distinct flavor, try fresh cilantro, dill, basil, parsley or green onions.

Balsamic or sherry vinegar (just a few drops) enhances the flavor of Brussels sprouts, cabbage, beans, carrots, onions and spinach. When you are not serving salad, try bottled ranch or Italian dressing on hot vegetables.

Sliced, slivered or chopped nuts add flavor and crunch to broccoli, asparagus, beans, celery, mashed squash or peas.

Quick Desserts

There's always time to prepare a dessert if you stock your freezer and pantry with ice cream, frozen fruits, canned fruits and pudding mixes. A little ingenuity dresses up these basic foods.

Melba Purée: Purée defrosted frozen raspberries and pour over fresh nectarines, strawberries or peaches, or drained canned fruit.

Mocha Fruit Freeze: Soften 1 pint ice cream at 30% (Medium Low) for 45 seconds to 1½ minutes, or until ice cream can be stirred smooth. Blend 1 tablespoon instant coffee crystals with 2 tablespoons water. Add to softened ice cream with whole or chopped frozen fruit.

Dessert à la Liqueur: Pour a splash of chilled liqueur, such as crème de menthe, curaçao or amaretto, over fresh fruit or ice cream.

Parfait Desserts: Layer pudding or ice cream in a parfait glass with one or two of the following: fresh or drained canned fruit, toasted coconut, chopped nuts, crumbled cookies, grated citrus rind, grated chocolate, whipped cream, granola.

Quick Bites

Gruyère Veggie Melt
Tuna-Veggie Potato Melts

Turkey Pizza Melt

Gruyère Veggie Melt

18

Presto Pizzas

Eight hot ideas in under 6 minutes!

A Presto Pizza contains no more than seven ingredients, microwaves in 5½ minutes or less and serves one. Each recipe calls for a particular type of bread, but the breads are interchangeable so you can substitute whatever you prefer or have on hand.

Use French or sourdough bread, English muffin, bagel or pita. If you create your own pizza combinations, be sure to select a flavorful, substantial bread with enough body to hold up under toppings. Toast the bread in a toaster or toaster oven to remove excess moisture and crisp it before microwaving.

How to Microwave Presto Pizzas

Toast bread in toaster or toaster oven.

Assemble pizza and place on paper towel in microwave oven.

Microwave as directed in recipe, or until hot and cheese is melted.

Turkey Pizza Melt

1 English muffin
6 green pepper strips (2½ × ¼-inch)
2 tablespoons pizza sauce
2 slices (1 oz. each) fully cooked turkey
2 slices (1 oz. each) mozzarella cheese

1 serving

Split and toast muffin. In small bowl, microwave pepper strips at High for 1 to 1½ minutes, or until tender. Spread muffin halves evenly with pizza sauce. Top each evenly with turkey, cheese and pepper strips. Place on paper towel. Microwave at High for 1 to 1½ minutes, or until muffin halves are hot and cheese is melted.

Per Serving: Calories: 431 • Protein: 40 g. • Carbohydrate: 37 g. • Fat: 13 g. • Cholesterol: 74 mg. • Sodium: 513 mg.
Exchanges: 2 starch, 4½ lean meat, 1½ vegetable

Gruyère Veggie Melt

1 bagel
½ cup quartered fresh mushrooms
1 tablespoon sliced green onion
¼ cup shredded Gruyère cheese
2 tablespoons seeded chopped tomato
Dash dried oregano leaves

1 serving

Split and toast bagel. In small bowl, combine mushrooms and onion. Microwave at High for 2 to 3 minutes, or until vegetables are tender, stirring once. Spoon evenly over bagel halves. Top evenly with cheese, tomato and oregano. Place on paper towel. Microwave at High for 2 to 2½ minutes, or until bagel halves are hot and cheese is melted, rotating once.

Per Serving: Calories: 230 • Protein: 15 g. • Carbohydrate: 34 g. • Fat: 11 g. • Cholesterol: 31 mg. • Sodium: 294 mg.
Exchanges: 2 starch, 1 vegetable, 1 medium-fat meat, 1 fat

Ham & Egg Muffin

Ham & Egg Muffin

1 English muffin
2 teaspoons prepared mustard
2 slices (1 oz. each) fully
   cooked ham
1 hard-cooked egg, sliced
1 to 2 tablespoons shredded
   fresh Parmesan cheese

1 serving

*Split and toast muffin. Spread evenly
with mustard. Top evenly with ham,
egg slices and cheese. Place on
paper towel. Microwave at High
for 1½ to 2 minutes, or until muffin
halves are hot and cheese is melted.*

Per Serving: Calories: 343 • Protein: 28 g.
• Carbohydrate: 33 g. • Fat: 10 g.
• Cholesterol: 249 mg. • Sodium: 987 mg.

Exchanges: 2 starch, 2 lean meat,
1 medium-fat meat

Cheddar Pears & Bacon Toast

1 slice sourdough bread, about
   ¾ inch thick
2 teaspoons mayonnaise
2 slices (1 oz. each) fully
   cooked Canadian bacon
½ medium pear, sliced
1 slice (1 oz.) Cheddar cheese

1 serving

*Toast bread and spread with may-
onnaise. Top with bacon, pear
slices and cheese. Place on paper
towel. Microwave at High for 1 to
2 minutes, or until bread is hot and
cheese is melted.*

Per Serving: Calories: 416 • Protein: 24 g.
• Carbohydrate: 29 g. • Fat: 23 g. •
Cholesterol: 69 mg. • Sodium: 1268 mg.

Exchanges: 1 starch, 3 medium-fat meat,
1 fruit, 1½ fat

Warm Chicken & Salsa-topped Pita

1 pita (4-inch)
2 teaspoons softened cream
   cheese
3 fresh spinach leaves
1 slice (1 oz.) fully cooked
   chicken or turkey
1 tablespoon salsa sauce

1 serving

*Split and toast pita. Spread evenly
with cream cheese. Top one half
with spinach leaves, chicken and
salsa. Top with remaining pita half.
Place on paper towel. Microwave
at High for 30 to 45 seconds, or
until hot.*

Per Serving: Calories: 154 • Protein: 11 g.
• Carbohydrate: 13 g. • Fat: 6 g. •
Cholesterol: 36 mg. • Sodium: 173 mg.

Exchanges: 1 starch, 1 medium-fat meat

*Cheddar Pears
& Bacon Toast*

*Warm Chicken &
Salsa-topped Pita*

21

Broccoli
Pepperoni
Toast

Mozzarella &
Tomato Pizza

22

Cheese & Bacon Melt

Mozzarella & Tomato Pizza

1 piece (4-inch) lengthwise-
  sliced French bread
2 teaspoons olive oil
¼ teaspoon dried basil leaves
  Dash salt
  Dash pepper
1 slice (1 oz.) mozzarella
  cheese, cut into 3 strips
1 Roma tomato, cut into 6
  slices

1 serving

Toast bread. In small bowl, combine oil, basil, salt and pepper. Mix well. Brush evenly over bread. Top with mozzarella strips and tomato slices, slightly overlapping. Place on paper towel. Microwave at High for 30 seconds to 1 minute, or until bread is hot and cheese is melted.

Per Serving: Calories: 273 • Protein: 12 g.
• Carbohydrate: 23 g. • Fat: 15 g. •
Cholesterol: 16 mg. • Sodium: 489 mg.
Exchanges: 1½ starch, 1 medium-fat meat,
2 fat

Broccoli Pepperoni Toast

1 piece (4-inch) lengthwise-
  sliced French bread
½ cup frozen broccoli cuts
8 slices pepperoni (1¼-inch
  diameter)
2 tablespoons spaghetti sauce
1 tablespoon shredded fresh
  Parmesan cheese

1 serving

Toast bread. In small mixing bowl, microwave broccoli at High for 1 to 2 minutes, or until tender-crisp. Arrange pepperoni on bread. Top with broccoli, spaghetti sauce and cheese. Place on paper towel. Microwave at High for 1½ to 2 minutes, or until bread is hot and cheese is melted.

Per Serving: Calories: 242 • Protein: 11 g.
• Carbohydrate: 27 g. • Fat: 10 g. •
Cholesterol: 17 mg. • Sodium: 834 mg.
Exchanges: 1 starch, ½ high-fat meat,
2½ vegetable, 1 fat

Cheese & Bacon Melt

1 slice sourdough bread, about
  ¾ inch thick
1 slice bacon
¼ cup shredded Monterey Jack
  cheese
½ small avocado, sliced

1 serving

Toast bread. Cut bacon slice in half. Place on paper-towel-lined plate. Microwave at High for 1½ to 2 minutes, or until crisp. Crumble bacon. Sprinkle cheese on bread. Top with bacon. Place on paper towel. Microwave at High for 30 to 45 seconds, or until bread is hot and cheese is melted. Top with avocado slices.

Per Serving: Calories: 405 • Protein: 14 g.
• Carbohydrate: 27 g. • Fat: 28 g. •
Cholesterol: 32 mg. • Sodium: 465 mg.
Exchanges: 1½ starch, 1 medium-fat meat,
4½ fat

Speed Spuds

A meal or snack in a potato!

Microwave speed gives baked potatoes a place in this collection of superfast foods. Medium-size potatoes take just minutes to microwave and stand. You can also use leftover cooked potatoes. Just split the refrigerated potato and microwave as directed in the reheating chart before adding toppings and returning to the microwave for final heating.

Some of these recipes include enough protein for a complete meal. Others make a tasty snack or substantial side dish. All call for no more than seven ingredients.

Potatoes with Dilled Chicken & Beans

Cooking Chart

Potato or Sweet Potato (8 to 10 oz. each)	Microwave at High
1	3 to 6½ minutes
2	5 to 10 minutes

Reheating Chart

Potato or Sweet Potato (8 to 10 oz. each), refrigerated	Microwave at High
1	2 to 3 minutes
2	3½ to 4 minutes

How to Microwave Speed Spuds

Pierce each potato with fork. Place on paper towel in microwave oven.

Microwave as directed in chart, turning over and rearranging potatoes once. Let stand for 5 minutes while you assemble topping ingredients.

Top potatoes as directed in recipe and microwave until hot.

Italian
Stuffed
Potato

Potatoes with Dilled Chicken & Beans

2 baking potatoes (8 to 10 oz. each)
½ cup frozen cut green beans
1 pkg. (6½ oz.) frozen creamed chicken
¼ teaspoon dried dill weed

2 servings

Prepare potatoes as directed, left. Place green beans in 1-quart casserole. Cover. Microwave at High for 2 to 4 minutes, or until hot. Remove creamed chicken from packaging and add to green beans. Sprinkle with dill weed. Re-cover. Microwave at High for 5 to 6 minutes, or until hot, stirring once. Place potatoes on individual serving plates. Split open. Spoon chicken mixture evenly over each potato.

Per Serving: Calories: 340 • Protein: 15 g. • Carbohydrate: 47 g. • Fat: 11 g. • Cholesterol: 0 • Sodium: 350 mg.

Exchanges: 2½ starch, 1 lean meat, 2 vegetable, 1 fat

Italian Stuffed Potato

1 baking potato (8 to 10 oz.)
¼ lb. fresh Italian sausage, crumbled
2 tablespoons spaghetti sauce
¼ cup shredded mozzarella cheese

1 serving

Prepare potato as directed, left. In 1-quart casserole, microwave sausage at High for 1½ to 2 minutes, or until no longer pink, stirring once to break apart. Drain. Add spaghetti sauce. Mix well. Place potato on plate. Split open. Spoon meat mixture over potato. Sprinkle evenly with cheese. Microwave at High for 1 to 1½ minutes, or until hot and cheese is melted, rotating once.

Per Serving: Calories: 457 • Protein: 24 g. • Carbohydrate: 47 g. • Fat: 19 g. • Cholesterol: 57 mg. • Sodium: 863 mg.

Exchanges: 2½ starch, 1½ medium-fat meat, 2 vegetable, 2 fat

Creamy
Broccoli-topped
Potato

Creamy Broccoli-topped Potato

1 baking potato (8 to 10 oz.)
½ cup frozen cut broccoli
¼ cup chive-and-onion-flavored
    sour cream
2 teaspoons diced pimiento

1 serving

Prepare potato as directed, page 24. Place broccoli in 1-quart casserole. Cover. Microwave at High for 1½ to 2 minutes, or until hot. Stir in sour cream. Place potato on plate. Split open. Spoon broccoli mixture over potato. Sprinkle with pimiento.

Per Serving: Calories: 325 • Protein: 8 g.
• Carbohydrate: 47 g. • Fat: 13 g. •
Cholesterol: 27 mg. • Sodium: 61 mg.
Exchanges: 2½ starch, 2 vegetable, 2 fat

Turkey-topped Potato

1 baking potato (8 to 10 oz.)
½ cup diced cooked turkey
3 tablespoons plain low-fat
    yogurt
2 tablespoons seeded
    chopped tomato
¼ teaspoon dried basil leaves
⅛ teaspoon garlic salt
    Avocado slices

1 serving

Prepare potato as directed, page 24. In small mixing bowl, combine turkey, yogurt, tomato, basil and garlic salt. Place potato on plate. Split open. Spoon turkey mixture over potato. Top with avocado slices.

Per Serving: Calories: 373 • Protein: 28 g.
• Carbohydrate: 47 g. • Fat: 8 g. •
Cholesterol: 56 mg. • Sodium: 323 mg.
Exchanges: 2½ starch, 2 lean meat,
1 vegetable, ½ low-fat milk

Potato with Black Beans & Salsa

1 baking potato (8 to 10 oz.)
¼ cup canned black beans,
    rinsed and drained
2 tablespoons salsa
¼ cup shredded Monterey Jack
    cheese

1 serving

Prepare potato as directed, page 24. Place potato on plate. Split open. Spoon beans over potato. Top with salsa and cheese. Microwave at High for 1 to 2 minutes, or until hot and cheese is melted.

Per Serving: Calories: 359 • Protein: 15 g.
• Carbohydrate: 55 g. • Fat: 9 g. •
Cholesterol: 25 mg. • Sodium: 395 mg.
Exchanges: 3 starch, 2 vegetable, 2 fat

Turkey-topped
Potato

Potato with Black
Beans & Salsa

27

*Spicy Tomato-sauced
Sweet Potatoes*

*Tuna-Veggie
Potato Melts*

Cheesy
Chili-topped
Potatoes

Tuna-Veggie Potato Melts

2 baking potatoes (8 to
    10 oz. each)
1 cup frozen broccoli,
    cauliflower and carrots
1 can (3¼ oz.) solid white
    tuna, water pack, drained
    and flaked
¼ teaspoon salt
½ cup shredded Cheddar
    cheese

2 servings

Prepare potatoes as directed, page 24. Place vegetables in 1-quart casserole. Cover. Microwave at High for 3 to 4 minutes, or until hot, stirring once. Add tuna and salt. Mix well. Place potatoes on individual serving plates. Split open. Spoon vegetable mixture evenly over each potato. Sprinkle with cheese. Microwave at High for 1½ to 3 minutes, or until cheese is melted, rotating once.

Per Serving: Calories: 368 • Protein: 25 g.
• Carbohydrate: 45 g. • Fat: 10 g. •
Cholesterol: 37 mg. • Sodium: 622 mg.
Exchanges: 2½ starch, 2 lean meat,
2 vegetable

Spicy Tomato-sauced Sweet Potatoes

2 sweet potatoes (8 to
    10 oz. each)
1 can (8 oz.) whole tomatoes,
    undrained and cut up
⅓ cup chopped green pepper
½ teaspoon chili powder
¼ teaspoon ground ginger
¼ teaspoon sugar
⅛ teaspoon salt

2 servings

Prepare potatoes as directed, page 24. In 2-cup measure, combine remaining ingredients. Microwave at High for 4 to 5 minutes, or until pepper is tender, stirring once.

Place potatoes on individual serving plates. Split open. Spoon tomato mixture evenly over each potato.

Per Serving: Calories: 272 • Protein: 5 g.
• Carbohydrate: 12 g. • Fat: 1 g. •
Cholesterol: 0 • Sodium: 356 mg.
Exchanges: 3 starch, 3 vegetable

Cheesy Chili-topped Potatoes

2 baking potatoes (8 to
    10 oz. each)
⅔ cup chili with beans
½ cup shredded Mexican
    pasteurized process
    cheese loaf
¼ cup shredded lettuce
¼ cup seeded chopped
    tomato

2 servings

Prepare potatoes as directed, page 24. Place potatoes on individual serving plates. Split open.

Spoon ⅓ cup chili evenly over each potato. Sprinkle evenly with cheese. Microwave at High for 1 to 2 minutes, or until chili is hot and cheese is melted, rotating once. Sprinkle each potato with lettuce and tomato.

Per Serving: Calories: 386 • Protein: 16 g.
• Carbohydrate: 53 g. • Fat: 14 g. •
Cholesterol: 41 mg. • Sodium: 864 mg.
Exchanges: 3 starch, 1 vegetable, 1 high-fat meat, 1 fat

Wrap-it Meals

*A meal in hand
in less than a minute!*

Tuna Sprout Foldover

The ultimate fast-and-easy snack or mini-meal for
someone on the go, a Wrap-it Meal takes no more
than four ingredients and microwaves in 1 minute or
less. If you don't have the type of bread suggested in
the recipe, substitute any of these pliable wraps: pita
folds, soft cracker bread, lefse, flour tortilla.

How to Microwave Wrap-it Meals

Spread wrap with filling. Place on
paper towel in microwave oven.

Microwave as directed in recipe,
or until hot.

Roll up wrap to enclose filling.

Chili Avocado Roll-up

Ham & Egg Roll-ups

Tuna Sprout Foldover

1 pita fold bread (7-inch)
¼ cup drained and flaked canned tuna
¼ cup shredded Cheddar cheese
¼ cup alfalfa sprouts

1 serving

Sprinkle center of pita fold evenly with tuna. Sprinkle evenly with cheese. Place on paper towel. Microwave at High for 45 seconds to 1 minute, or until hot and cheese is melted. Top with sprouts. Roll up or fold over pita, enclosing filling.

Per Serving: Calories: 276 • Protein: 24 g. • Carbohydrate: 20 g. • Fat: 11 g. • Cholesterol: 37 mg. • Sodium: 327 mg. Exchanges: 1 starch, 2½ medium-fat meat, 1 vegetable

Ham & Egg Roll-ups

½ sheet lefse (13-inch)
1 tablespoon soft chive and pimiento cream cheese spread
1 slice (1 oz.) thinly sliced fully cooked ham
1 hard-cooked egg, chopped

1 serving

Spread lefse evenly with cream cheese. Place ham slice over cream cheese. Sprinkle with egg. Place on paper towel. Microwave at High for 45 seconds to 1 minute, or until hot. Roll up lefse, enclosing filling.

Per Serving: Calories: 256 • Protein: 16 g. • Carbohydrate: 17 g. • Fat: 13 g. • Cholesterol: 245 mg. • Sodium: 575 mg. Exchanges: 1 starch, 2 medium-fat meat, ½ fat

Chili Avocado Roll-up

1 flour tortilla (8-inch)
¼ cup canned chili with beans
1 tablespoon picante sauce
2 tablespoons chopped avocado

1 serving

Spread center of tortilla evenly with chili. Top evenly with picante sauce. Place on paper towel. Microwave at High for 45 seconds to 1 minute, or until hot. Sprinkle avocado over chili and sauce. Roll up tortilla, enclosing filling.

Per Serving: Calories: 204 • Protein: 6 g. • Carbohydrate: 27 g. • Fat: 9 g. • Cholesterol: 11 mg. • Sodium: 584 mg. Exchanges: 1½ starch, 1 vegetable, 1½ fat

Scandinavian
Roll-ups

Cheese, Chili &
Tomato Roll-up

Cheese, Chili & Tomato Roll-up

  1 flour tortilla (8-inch)
 ¼ cup shredded Co-Jack cheese
  1 tablespoon canned chopped green chilies
  2 tablespoons seeded chopped tomato

1 serving

Sprinkle center of tortilla evenly with cheese. Top with chilies. Place on paper towel. Microwave at High for 45 seconds to 1 minute, or until hot and cheese is melted. Sprinkle tomato over cheese and chilies. Roll up tortilla, enclosing filling.

Per Serving: Calories: 213 • Protein: 9 g. • Carbohydrate: 20 g.
• Fat: 11 g. • Cholesterol: 26 mg. • Sodium: 462 mg.
Exchanges: 1 starch, 1 medium-fat meat, 1 vegetable, 1 fat

Scandinavian Roll-ups

 ½ sheet lefse (13-inch)
  1 to 2 tablespoons softened cream cheese
  1 can (3⅓ oz.) skinless, boneless salmon,
     rinsed and drained
  1 tablespoon sweet pickle relish

1 serving

Spread lefse evenly with cream cheese. Spoon salmon evenly down center. Top with pickle relish. Place on paper towel. Microwave at High for 45 seconds to 1 minute, or until hot. Roll up lefse, enclosing filling.

Per Serving: Calories: 278 • Protein: 20 g. • Carbohydrate: 21 g.
• Fat: 12 g. • Cholesterol: 50 mg. • Sodium: 693 mg.
Exchanges: 1 starch, 2 medium-fat meat, 1 vegetable, ½ fat

Chicken Barbecue Roll-ups

Beef & Guacamole Roll-up

Chicken Barbecue Roll-ups

¼ sheet soft cracker bread (15-inch)
1 tablespoon barbecue sauce
1 slice (1 oz.) thinly sliced fully cooked chicken
   or turkey
¼ cup shredded lettuce

1 serving

Spread cracker bread evenly with barbecue sauce. Place chicken slice in center over sauce. Place on paper towel. Microwave at High for 45 seconds to 1 minute, or until hot. Top with lettuce. Roll up cracker bread, enclosing filling.

Per Serving: Calories: 180 • Protein: 12 g. • Carbohydrate: 22 g. • Fat: 4 g. • Cholesterol: 25 mg. • Sodium: 315 mg.
Exchanges: 1 starch, 1 lean meat, 1½ vegetable

Beef & Guacamole Roll-up

1 flour tortilla (8-inch)
1 tablespoon frozen avocado guacamole,
   defrosted
2 slices (1 oz. each) thinly sliced fully cooked
   roast beef
2 slices (1 oz. each) thinly sliced Monterey Jack
   cheese

1 serving

Spread center of tortilla evenly with guacamole. Top with roast beef and cheese. Place on paper towel. Microwave at High for 45 seconds to 1 minute, or until hot and cheese is melted. Roll up tortilla, enclosing filling.

Per Serving: Calories: 460 • Protein: 35 g. • Carbohydrate: 19 g. • Fat: 27 g. • Cholesterol: 105 mg. • Sodium: 568 mg.
Exchanges: 1 starch, 4 medium-fat meat, 1 vegetable, 1 fat

Pasta Pronto

Fast, no-fuss gourmet pasta!

These pasta meals for two can be ready in 12 minutes or less. The secret is fresh pasta, cooked conventionally while you microwave a sauce. Once the water boils, you can cook fresh pasta in 45 seconds to 3 minutes. Look for it in the deli or refrigerator section of the supermarket.

If you don't have fresh pasta on hand, you can still prepare these meals quickly. Try a microwave pasta product or dry cappelini or vermicelli, which cook in under 5 minutes.

Broccoli-Cheese Pasta with Ham

The fastest pasta meal of all is one you make with leftover cooked pasta. To save extra unsauced pasta for a future meal, toss it with a little vegetable or olive oil before you refrigerate it. This keeps the pasta from sticking together in a solid mass as it cools. To reheat 2 cups of cold pasta, microwave, covered, 1½ to 2 minutes at High.

How to Microwave Pasta Pronto

Cook pasta conventionally, as directed on the package.

Microwave sauce as directed in recipe, or until hot.

Toss or top hot, drained pasta with sauce.

Lemon Basil Shrimp & Ravioli

Broccoli-Cheese Pasta with Ham

4 oz. uncooked fresh linguine
1 pkg. (10 oz.) frozen broccoli in cheese-flavored
   sauce
2 slices (1 oz. each) fully cooked ham, cut
   into ¾-inch pieces

2 servings

Prepare linguine as directed on package. Rinse and drain. Set aside. Place broccoli in cheese sauce in 1½-quart casserole. Cover. Microwave at High for 6 to 8 minutes, or until hot, stirring once. Add linguine and ham. Toss to coat. Re-cover. Microwave at High for 2 to 3 minutes, or until hot, stirring once.

Per Serving: Calories: 338 • Protein: 17 g. • Carbohydrate: 55 g.
• Fat: 5 g. • Cholesterol: 15 mg. • Sodium: 1006 mg.
Exchanges: 3 starch, 1 medium-fat meat, 2 vegetable

Lemon Basil Shrimp & Ravioli

4 oz. uncooked fresh cheese ravioli
1 tablespoon margarine or butter
½ teaspoon grated lemon peel
¼ teaspoon dried basil leaves
1 tablespoon lemon juice
1 pkg. (6 oz.) frozen cooked shrimp, defrosted

2 servings

Prepare ravioli as directed on package. Rinse and drain. Set aside. In 1½-quart casserole, combine margarine, lemon peel and basil. Microwave at High for 45 seconds to 1 minute, or until margarine is melted. Add lemon juice. Mix well. Add ravioli and shrimp. Toss to coat. Cover. Microwave at High for 2 to 3½ minutes, or until hot.

Per Serving: Calories: 308 • Protein: 27 g. • Carbohydrate: 28 g.
• Fat: 9 g. • Cholesterol: 197 mg. • Sodium: 518 mg.
Exchanges: 2 starch, 3 lean meat

Cheese
& Mushroom
Pasta

Cheese & Mushroom Pasta

4 oz. uncooked fresh fettucini
1 cup sliced fresh mushrooms
1 tablespoon margarine or
   butter
1 teaspoon freeze-dried chives
1 teaspoon Worcestershire
   sauce
4 oz. pasteurized process
   American cheese loaf, cut
   into ½-inch cubes (½ cup)

2 servings

Prepare fettucini as directed on package. Rinse and drain. Set aside. In 1½-quart casserole, combine mushrooms, margarine, chives and Worcestershire sauce. Cover. Microwave at High for 1½ to 2 minutes, or until mushrooms are tender. Add cheese. Microwave at High, uncovered, for 2 to 2½ minutes, or until cheese is melted, stirring twice. Add fettucini. Toss to coat. Microwave at High for 1½ to 2 minutes, or until hot.

Per Serving: Calories: 459 • Protein: 19 g.
• Carbohydrate: 49 g. • Fat: 21 g. •
Cholesterol: 36 mg. • Sodium: 771 mg.
Exchanges: 3 starch, 1 high-fat meat,
1 vegetable, 2 fat

Herb-Garlic Pasta

4 oz. uncooked fresh fettucini
3 tablespoons margarine or
   butter
1 clove garlic, minced
2 tablespoons grated
   Parmesan cheese
1 teaspoon dried parsley flakes
¼ teaspoon dried basil leaves
⅛ teaspoon coarsely ground
   pepper

2 servings

Prepare fettucini as directed on package. Rinse and drain. Set aside. In 1½-quart casserole, place margarine and garlic. Cover. Microwave at High for 1 to 1¼ minutes, or until margarine is melted. Stir in remaining ingredients. Re-cover. Microwave at High for 1 minute. Mix well. Add fettucini. Toss to coat. Cover. Microwave at High for 1½ to 2 minutes, or until hot. Sprinkle with additional grated Parmesan cheese, if desired.

Per Serving: Calories: 396 • Protein: 10 g.
• Carbohydrate: 44 g. • Fat: 20 g. •
Cholesterol: 5 mg. • Sodium: 320 mg.
Exchanges: 3 starch, 4 fat

Quick Cacciatore Pasta

4 oz. uncooked fresh fettucini
1 prepackaged and marinated
   chicken breast (5 oz.), cut
   into 1-inch pieces
1 cup spaghetti sauce
½ cup green pepper strips
   (2 × ¼-inch)
½ cup sliced onion, separated
   into rings

2 servings

Prepare fettucini as directed on package. Rinse and drain. Set aside. Place chicken in 1½-quart casserole. Cover with wax paper or microwave cooking paper. Microwave at High for 1½ to 2 minutes, or until chicken is no longer pink, rearranging once. Drain. Add spaghetti sauce, pepper and onion. Mix well. Re-cover. Microwave at High for 3 to 4 minutes, or until vegetables are tender and sauce is hot. Serve over fettucini.

Per Serving: Calories: 456 • Protein: 25 g.
• Carbohydrate: 70 g. • Fat: 9 g. •
Cholesterol: 33 mg. • Sodium: 791 mg.
Exchanges: 3 starch, 2 lean meat,
5 vegetable

Herb-Garlic Pasta

Quick Cacciatore Pasta

37

Quick
Pizza Pasta

Italian Pasta
Toss

Quick Pizza Pasta

4 oz. uncooked fresh fettucini
1 cup pizza sauce
¼ cup sliced, quartered zucchini
1 tablespoon water
12 slices pepperoni
1 tablespoon grated Parmesan cheese

2 servings

Prepare fettucini as directed on package. Rinse and drain. Set aside. In 1½-quart casserole, combine pizza sauce, zucchini and water. Cover. Microwave at High for 1½ to 2 minutes, or until zucchini is tender-crisp, stirring once. Add fettucini and pepperoni. Toss to coat. Re-cover. Microwave at High for 1½ to 2 minutes, or until hot. Sprinkle with cheese.

Per Serving: Calories: 372 • Protein: 13 g. • Carbohydrate: 56 g. • Fat: 10 g. • Cholesterol: 14 mg. • Sodium: 1044 mg.
Exchanges: 3 starch, 2 vegetable, 2 fat

Italian Pasta Toss

4 oz. uncooked fresh fettucini
⅓ cup sliced onion, separated into rings
3 tablespoons margarine or butter
1 clove garlic, minced
2 Roma tomatoes, each cut into 6 wedges
½ cup sliced zucchini
¼ teaspoon dried basil leaves

2 servings

Prepare fettucini as directed on package. Rinse and drain. Set aside. In 1½-quart casserole, combine onion rings, margarine and garlic. Cover. Microwave at High for 1½ to 2 minutes, or until onions are tender. Add tomatoes, zucchini and basil. Mix well. Add fettucini. Toss to coat. Re-cover. Microwave at High for 1½ to 2 minutes, or until hot.

Per Serving: Calories: 389 • Protein: 9 g. • Carbohydrate: 49 g. • Fat: 18 g. • Cholesterol: 0 • Sodium: 209 mg.
Exchanges: 3 starch, 1 vegetable, 3 fat

Tortellini with
Rosemary & Garlic

Veggies &
Pasta

Tortellini with Rosemary & Garlic

    4 oz. uncooked fresh cheese tortellini
    ½ cup green and red pepper strips (2 × ¼-inch)
    2 tablespoons olive oil
    1 clove garlic, minced
    ¼ teaspoon dried rosemary leaves, crushed
    2 teaspoons white wine vinegar

2 servings

*Prepare tortellini as directed on package. Rinse and
drain. Set aside. In 1½-quart casserole, combine
pepper strips, oil, garlic and rosemary. Cover. Microwave at High for 2 to 3 minutes, or until peppers are
tender-crisp. Stir in vinegar. Add tortellini. Toss to coat.
Re-cover. Microwave at High for 1 to 2 minutes, or
until hot.*

Per Serving: Calories: 302 • Protein: 9 g. • Carbohydrate: 29 g.
• Fat: 17 g. • Cholesterol: 31 mg. • Sodium: 262 mg.
Exchanges: 2 starch, ½ high-fat meat, 2 fat

Veggies & Pasta

    4 oz. uncooked fresh linguine
    1 pkg. (9 oz.) frozen broccoli, cauliflower
       and carrots in butter sauce
    ¼ teaspoon dried thyme leaves
    1 tablespoon grated Romano or Parmesan
       cheese

2 servings

*Prepare linguine as directed on package. Rinse and
drain. Set aside. Place vegetables in 1½-quart casserole. Cover. Microwave at High for 6 to 8 minutes, or
until hot, stirring once. Add linguine and thyme. Toss
to coat. Re-cover. Microwave at High for 1½ to 2
minutes, or until hot. Sprinkle with cheese.*

Per Serving: Calories: 274 • Protein: 10 g. • Carbohydrate: 50 g.
• Fat: 4 g. • Cholesterol: 3 mg. • Sodium: 395 mg.
Exchanges: 2½ starch, 2½ vegetable, ½ fat

Mornay
Spinach Fettucini

Roasted Red
Pepper &
Basil Pasta

40

Creamy Bacon & Pasta Dish

Roasted Red Pepper & Basil Pasta

- 4 oz. uncooked fresh linguine
- ⅓ cup whipping cream
- 2 tablespoons margarine or butter
- 1 clove garlic, minced
- ¼ cup roasted red pepper, drained and sliced
- 2 tablespoons grated Parmesan cheese
- ¼ cup sliced black olives

2 servings

Prepare linguine as directed on package. Rinse and drain. Set aside. In 1½-quart casserole, combine cream, margarine and garlic. Microwave at High for 1½ to 2 minutes, or until margarine is melted, stirring once. Add red pepper and cheese. Mix well. Microwave at High for 2 to 3 minutes, or until mixture is slightly thickened, stirring once. Add linguine. Toss to coat. Microwave at High for 1½ to 2 minutes, or until hot. Sprinkle with olives.

Per Serving: Calories: 506 • Protein: 11 g. • Carbohydrate: 46 g. • Fat: 31 g. • Cholesterol: 59 mg. • Sodium: 405 mg. Exchanges: 3 starch, ½ vegetable, 6 fat

Mornay Spinach Fettucini

- 4 oz. uncooked fresh spinach fettucini
- 1½ cups frozen mixed vegetables
- ¾ cup milk
- 1 pkg. (0.87 oz.) white sauce mix
- 2 tablespoons grated Parmesan cheese
- ½ teaspoon dried parsley flakes
- 2 tablespoons dry sherry
- 2 tablespoons finely shredded Swiss cheese

2 servings

Prepare fettucini as directed on package. Rinse and drain. Set aside. Place vegetables in 1½-quart casserole. Cover. Microwave at High for 6 to 7 minutes, or until vegetables are defrosted, stirring once. Drain. Add remaining ingredients, except Swiss cheese. Mix well. Microwave at High, uncovered, for 6 to 8 minutes, or until mixture thickens and bubbles, stirring twice. Serve sauce over fettucini. Sprinkle with cheese.

Per Serving: Calories: 544 • Protein: 23 g. • Carbohydrate: 75 g. • Fat: 16 g. • Cholesterol: 25 mg. • Sodium: 1116 mg. Exchanges: 4 starch, ½ high-fat meat, ½ low-fat milk, 2 vegetable, 1½ fat

Creamy Bacon & Pasta Dish

- 4 oz. uncooked fresh linguine
- 4 slices bacon, cut into ¾-inch pieces
- 1 cup frozen peas, defrosted
- ¼ cup whipping cream
- 2 tablespoons grated Romano cheese
- 1 tablespoon margarine or butter
- ¼ teaspoon dried marjoram leaves

2 servings

Prepare linguine as directed on package. Rinse and drain. Set aside. Place bacon in 1½-quart casserole. Cover with paper towel. Microwave bacon at High for 4 to 8 minutes, or until brown and crisp, stirring once to break apart. Drain. Add remaining ingredients. Mix well. Microwave at High for 1½ to 2 minutes, or until mixture is thickened, stirring once. Add cooked linguine. Toss to coat. Microwave at High for 1½ to 2 minutes, or until hot. Sprinkle with Romano or Parmesan cheese, if desired.

Per Serving: Calories: 517 • Protein: 17 g. • Carbohydrate: 54 g. • Fat: 26 g. • Cholesterol: 58 mg. • Sodium: 437 mg. Exchanges: 3½ starch, 1 high-fat meat, 3½ fat

Fast Fish

An entreé for two in 10 minutes or less!

Microwaving is an excellent method for cooking fish or vegetables. Put these foods together in delicious combinations of no more than seven ingredients, and you get a complete meal for two that microwaves in 10 minutes or less.

How to Microwave Fast Fish

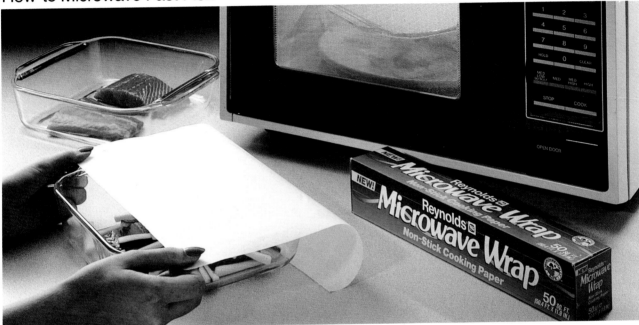

Arrange fish fillets or pieces in 8-inch square baking dish.

Prepare remaining ingredients. Spoon evenly over fillets and cover with wax paper or microwave cooking paper.

Microwave as directed in recipe, or until fish flakes easily with fork, rearranging once.

Salmon with Mustard Ranch Sauce

1 salmon fillet (about 8 oz.), cut in half crosswise
1 small zucchini, cut into 2 × ½-inch lengths (about ¾ cup)
⅛ teaspoon salt
⅛ teaspoon pepper
8 cherry tomatoes, halved
¼ cup ranch dressing
2 teaspoons prepared mustard

2 servings

Arrange fillet halves, skin-sides-down, in 8-inch square baking dish. Top evenly with zucchini. Sprinkle with salt and pepper. Cover with wax paper or microwave cooking paper. Microwave at 70% (Medium High) for 6 to 9 minutes, or until fish flakes easily with fork, rearranging once. Add tomatoes. Re-cover. Microwave at High for 45 seconds to 1 minute, or until tomatoes are warm. In small bowl, combine dressing and mustard. Top fish with dressing.

Per Serving: Calories: 284 • Protein: 24 g. • Carbohydrate: 6 g. • Fat: 18 g.
• Cholesterol: 64 mg. • Sodium: 473 mg.
Exchanges: 3 lean meat, 1 vegetable, 2 fat

*Sole with
Mustard-Dill Butter*

Sole with
Mustard-Dill Butter

- 2 sole fillets (about 4 oz. each)
- 3 tablespoons margarine or
     butter
- 2 teaspoons Dijon mustard
- ¼ teaspoon dried dill weed
     Dash pepper

2 servings

*Arrange fillets in 8-inch square bak-
ing dish. Set aside. In small mixing
bowl, microwave margarine at 30%
(Medium Low) for 15 to 30 seconds,
or until softened. Add remaining
ingredients. Mix well. Spread mixture evenly over fillets. Cover with
wax paper or microwave cooking
paper. Microwave at High for 5 to
7 minutes, or until fish flakes easily
with fork, rearranging once.*

Per Serving: Calories: 263 • Protein: 22 g.
• Carbohydrate: 0 • Fat: 19 g. •
Cholesterol: 54 mg. • Sodium: 440 mg.
Exchanges: 3 lean meat, 2 fat

Lemony Sole
& Vegetables

- 2 sole fillets (about 4 oz. each)
- 20 fresh pea pods (about 2 oz.)
- ⅓ cup julienne carrot (2 × ⅛-
     inch strips)
- 1 tablespoon margarine or
     butter, cut into small pieces
- 1 teaspoon grated lemon peel
- 2 teaspoons fresh lemon juice

2 servings

*Arrange fillets in 8-inch square
baking dish. Top evenly with remaining ingredients. Cover with
wax paper or microwave cooking
paper. Microwave at High for 5 to
7 minutes, or until fish flakes easily
with fork, rearranging once.*

Per Serving: Calories: 182 • Protein: 23 g.
• Carbohydrate: 6 g. • Fat: 7 g. •
Cholesterol: 54 mg. • Sodium: 169 mg.
Exchanges: 3 lean meat, 1½ vegetable

Peachy Sweet-Sour Sole

- 2 sole fillets (about 4 oz. each)
- 2 tablespoons peach
     preserves
- 2 tablespoons chili sauce
- ½ teaspoon cayenne
- ½ teaspoon white vinegar

2 servings

*Arrange fillets in 8-inch square
baking dish. Set aside. In small
mixing bowl, combine remaining
ingredients. Spoon mixture evenly
over fillets. Cover with wax paper
or microwave cooking paper. Microwave at High for 5 to 7 minutes, or
until fish flakes easily with fork, rearranging once.*

Per Serving: Calories: 171 • Protein: 22 g.
• Carbohydrate: 17 g. • Fat: 1 g. •
Cholesterol: 54 mg. • Sodium: 322 mg.
Exchanges: 3 lean meat, 1 fruit

Lemony Sole & Vegetables

Peachy Sweet-Sour Sole

*Zesty Sole
with Summer Squash*

*Lemon-Herb
Salmon Fillets*

Orange-sauced Roughy

Lemon-Herb Salmon Fillets

1 salmon fillet (about 8 oz.), cut in half crosswise
1 tablespoon margarine or butter
2 teaspoons lemon juice
¼ teaspoon hot pepper sauce
¼ teaspoon dried tarragon or marjoram leaves or dill weed
⅛ teaspoon salt

2 servings

Arrange fillet halves, skin-sides-down, in 8-inch square baking dish. Set aside. In small mixing bowl, microwave margarine at High for 45 seconds to 1 minute, or until melted. Stir in remaining ingredients. Spoon half of mixture evenly over salmon. Cover with wax paper or microwave cooking paper. Microwave at 70% (Medium High) for 5 to 7 minutes, or until fish flakes easily with fork, rearranging and spooning remaining margarine mixture over fish after half the cooking time.

Per Serving: Calories: 214 • Protein: 23 g.
• Carbohydrate: 1 g. • Fat: 13 g.
• Cholesterol: 62 mg. • Sodium: 255 mg.
Exchanges: 3 lean meat, 1 fat

Zesty Sole with Summer Squash

2 sole fillets (about 4 oz. each)
¼ cup chopped green pepper
¼ cup catsup
1 tablespoon prepared horseradish
2 teaspoons lemon juice
1 small yellow summer squash, sliced (about 1 cup)

2 servings

Arrange fillets in 8-inch square baking dish. Set aside. In small mixing bowl, combine pepper, catsup, horseradish and lemon juice. Spoon all but 1 tablespoon sauce over fillets. Top with squash slices. Spread remaining 1 tablespoon sauce over squash. Cover with wax paper or microwave cooking paper. Microwave at High for 7 to 9 minutes, or until fish flakes easily with fork, rearranging once.

Per Serving: Calories: 158 • Protein: 23 g.
• Carbohydrate: 13 g. • Fat: 2 g.
• Cholesterol: 54 mg. • Sodium: 456 mg.
Exchanges: 3 lean meat, 2½ vegetable

Orange-sauced Roughy

1 orange roughy fillet (about 8 oz.), cut in half crosswise
1 can (11 oz.) mandarin orange segments, drained
1 teaspoon cornstarch
¼ teaspoon salt
¼ teaspoon dried basil leaves
¼ cup orange juice
2 tablespoons sliced green onion

2 servings

Arrange fillet halves in 8-inch square baking dish. Top evenly with orange segments. Set aside. In small mixing bowl, combine cornstarch, salt, basil and orange juice. Add onion. Mix well. Pour over fish and oranges. Cover with wax paper or microwave cooking paper. Microwave at High for 6 to 10 minutes, or until fish flakes easily with fork, rearranging once.

Per Serving: Calories: 211 • Protein: 18 g.
• Carbohydrate: 17 g. • Fat: 8 g. •
Cholesterol: 23 mg. • Sodium: 341 mg.
Exchanges: 3 lean meat, 1 fruit

47

*Open-face Beef
& Mozzarella Sandwich*

Beef

Salsa-topped
Cubed Steaks

1 medium tomato, seeded and chopped (about 1 cup)
½ cup chopped green pepper
1 tablespoon canned sliced jalapeño peppers, drained and chopped
½ teaspoon sugar
½ teaspoon garlic salt
¼ teaspoon dried oregano leaves
½ cup frozen corn
4 beef cubed steaks (3 to 4 oz. each)

4 servings

In 2-cup measure, combine tomato, peppers, sugar, garlic salt and oregano. Microwave at High for 4 to 6 minutes, or until peppers are tender. Add corn. Mix well. Set aside.

Place cubed steaks in 10-inch square casserole. Cover. Microwave at High for 2 minutes. Turn cubed steaks. Microwave at High for 3 to 4 minutes, or until outside edges are no longer pink. Drain.

Spoon tomato mixture over cubed steaks. Re-cover. Microwave at 70% (Medium High) for 5 to 7 minutes, or until cubed steaks are tender.

Per Serving: Calories: 176 • Protein: 25 g.
• Carbohydrate: 7 g. • Fat: 5 g.
• Cholesterol: 64 mg. • Sodium: 332 mg.
Exchanges: 3 lean meat, 1½ vegetable

Salsa-topped Cubed Steaks

Mixed Green Salad
Corn Bread Muffins

Corned Beef & Broccoli Quiche

½ pkg. (15 oz.) refrigerated
    prepared pie crusts
2 cups frozen broccoli cuts
2 tablespoons all-purpose flour
⅓ cup milk
4 eggs
1 cup diced fully cooked
    corned beef (about 8 oz.)
1 jar (2 oz.) diced pimiento,
    drained
½ cup shredded Monterey Jack
    cheese

4 to 6 servings

Prepare pie crust as directed on package for single crust. Cool slightly. Place broccoli in 1-quart casserole. Cover. Microwave at High for 3 to 5 minutes, or until hot, stirring once. Drain. Set aside.

In medium mixing bowl, combine flour and milk. Blend until smooth. Beat in eggs. Stir in corned beef, pimiento and broccoli. Pour mixture into prepared crust. Cover with wax paper or microwave cooking paper.

Place pie plate on saucer in microwave oven. Microwave at 70% (Medium High) for 7 to 9 minutes, or until center is set. Sprinkle with cheese. Re-cover. Microwave at High for 30 seconds to 1 minute, or until cheese is melted. Let stand, covered, for 5 minutes.

Per Serving: Calories: 561 • Protein: 20 g. • Carbohydrate: 36 g. • Fat: 37 g. • Cholesterol: 189 mg. • Sodium: 970 mg.
Exchanges: 2 starch, 2 medium-fat meat, 1 vegetable, 5 fat

Corned Beef & Broccoli Quiche

Mixed Green Salad   *Fresh Fruit*

Open-face Beef & Mozzarella Sandwich

2 hoagie buns (6 to 7-inch), split
¼ cup chives and onion cream cheese spread
1½ cups quartered fresh mushrooms
½ cup sliced green onions
1 medium tomato, thinly sliced
8 slices fully cooked roast beef (½ to ¾ oz. each)
½ cup shredded mozzarella cheese

4 servings

Spread each bun half with 1 tablespoon cream cheese. Place on paper-towel-lined plate. Set aside.

In 1-quart casserole, combine mushrooms and onions. Cover. Microwave at High for 2 to 3 minutes, or until tender, stirring once. Drain.

Arrange tomato slices evenly on each bun half. Top evenly with roast beef slices and mushroom-onion mixture. Sprinkle each bun half evenly with cheese. Microwave at 70% (Medium High) for 3 to 4 minutes, or until cheese is melted.

Per Serving: Calories: 226 • Protein: 17 g. • Carbohydrate: 14 g. • Fat: 11 g.
• Cholesterol: 52 mg. • Sodium: 236 mg.
Exchanges: ½ starch, 1½ medium-fat meat, 1½ vegetable, 1 fat

Open-face Beef & Mozzarella Sandwich

Fruit Salad   Chocolate Chip Cookies

Oriental Sauced Patties ▶

1 lb. ground beef, crumbled
3 tablespoons soy sauce, divided
½ teaspoon garlic powder
½ cup sliced celery
2 tablespoons packed brown sugar
1 tablespoon cornstarch
2 tablespoons cider vinegar
1 can (8 oz.) pineapple chunks in juice, drained (reserve juice)

4 servings

Per Serving: Calories: 298 • Protein: 19 g. • Carbohydrate: 20 g. • Fat: 16 g.
• Cholesterol: 68 mg. • Sodium: 851 mg.
Exchanges: 2½ medium-fat meat, 1 vegetable, 1 fruit, ½ fat

Oriental Sauced Patties

Buttered Egg Noodles   Fortune Cookies & Lemon Sherbet

How to Microwave Oriental Sauced Patties

Combine ground beef, 1 tablespoon soy sauce and the garlic powder in medium mixing bowl. Divide mixture into 4 equal portions and shape each into 4-inch round patty.

Place patties on roasting rack. Cover with wax paper or microwave cooking paper. Microwave at High for 6 to 7 minutes, or until meat is firm and no longer pink, turning patties once during cooking. Set aside.

Place celery in 1-quart casserole. Microwave at High for 1 to 1½ minutes, or until tender. In 1-cup measure, combine sugar, cornstarch, vinegar and remaining 2 tablespoons soy sauce. Add to celery.

Add water to pineapple juice to equal ½ cup. Add to celery mixture. Microwave at High for 2½ to 5 minutes, or until mixture is thickened and translucent. Stir in pineapple. Spoon sauce over patties.

Hot & Spicy Cheeseburger

.1 lb. ground beef, crumbled
⅓ cup finely chopped onion
¼ cup chili sauce
2 tablespoons canned sliced
  jalapeño peppers, drained
  and finely chopped
4 slices Mexican pasteurized
  process cheese loaf (¼-
  inch slices)
4 hamburger buns

4 servings

In medium mixing bowl, combine ground beef, onion, chili sauce and peppers. Divide mixture into 4 equal portions and shape each into 4-inch round patty. Place patties on roasting rack.

Microwave at High for 6 to 9 minutes, or until meat is firm and no longer pink, turning patties once during cooking. Top each with cheese slice. Microwave at High for 30 seconds to 1½ minutes, or until cheese is melted. Let stand for 1 to 2 minutes. Serve on buns.

Per Serving: Calories: 470 • Protein: 29 g. • Carbohydrate: 27 g. • Fat: 27 g. • Cholesterol: 98 mg. • Sodium: 900 mg.
Exchanges: 1 starch, 3 medium-fat meat, 2 vegetable, 2½ fat

Hot & Spicy Cheeseburger

Cucumber Potato Salad, page 111   *Peanut Date Bars, page 148*

Cubed Steaks with Creamed Potatoes & Peas

12 oz. new potatoes, sliced (about 2 cups)
2 tablespoons water
1 pkg. (10 oz.) frozen creamed peas
¼ teaspoon dried marjoram leaves
⅛ teaspoon pepper
4 beef cubed steaks (3 to 4 oz. each)

4 servings

In 1½-quart casserole, combine potatoes and water. Cover. Microwave at High for 4 to 6 minutes, or until potatoes are tender-crisp. Drain. Add peas, marjoram and pepper. Re-cover. Microwave at High for 3 to 6 minutes, or until peas are defrosted. Set aside.

Place cubed steaks in 10-inch square casserole. Cover. Microwave at High for 2 minutes. Turn cubed steaks over. Microwave at High for 3 to 4 minutes, or until outside edges are no longer pink. Drain.

Spoon potato mixture over cubed steaks. Re-cover. Microwave at 70% (Medium High) for 5 to 7 minutes, or until cubed steaks are tender.

Per Serving: Calories: 323 • Protein: 30 g. • Carbohydrate: 28 g. • Fat: 10 g. • Cholesterol: 65 mg. • Sodium: 395 mg.
Exchanges: 2 starch, 3 lean meat

Cubed Steaks with Creamed Potatoes & Peas

Crisp Lettuce Salad   Dinner Rolls

Speedy Texan Chili

1 lb. boneless beef sirloin,
   about 1 inch thick, cut into
   thin strips
1 can (16 oz.) whole tomatoes,
   undrained and cut up
1 jar (8 oz.) taco sauce (1 cup)
1 medium green pepper, cut
   into 1-inch chunks
1 teaspoon chili powder
1 teaspoon sugar
¼ teaspoon salt
   Tortilla chips

4 servings

In 2-quart casserole, combine all ingredients, except tortilla chips. Cover. Microwave at 70% (Medium High) for 12 to 20 minutes, or until meat is no longer pink and pepper is tender-crisp, stirring twice. Serve with tortilla chips.

Per Serving: Calories: 208 • Protein: 24 g. • Carbohydrate: 11 g. • Fat: 7 g. • Cholesterol: 66 mg. • Sodium: 740 mg.
Exchanges: 3 lean meat, 2 vegetable

Speedy Texan Chili

Corn Bread Sticks with Honey Butter
Vanilla Ice Cream with Strawberries & Chocolate Sauce

Beef & Onion Fajitas

½ cup Italian dressing
2 tablespoons lime juice
1 teaspoon packed brown
     sugar
1 cup sliced red onion
1 cup sliced green pepper
12 oz. fully cooked roast beef,
     cut into thin strips (½-inch)
4 flour tortillas (8-inch)
     Sour cream
     Guacamole

4 servings

In 2-quart casserole, combine
dressing, lime juice and sugar.
Add onion and pepper. Mix well.
Cover. Microwave at High for 2 to
5 minutes, or until vegetables are
tender-crisp, stirring once.

Add beef. Mix well. Re-cover.
Microwave at High for 2 to 4 min-
utes, or until hot, stirring once.
Set aside.

Place tortillas between 2 damp-
ened paper towels. Microwave at
High for 30 seconds to 1 minute,
or just until tortillas are warm to
the touch.

Spoon one-fourth of beef mixture
down center of each tortilla. Roll
up tortillas to enclose filling. Top
with sour cream and guacamole.

Per Serving: Calories: 468 • Protein: 30 g.
• Carbohydrate: 26 g. • Fat: 27 g.
• Cholesterol: 84 mg. • Sodium: 455 mg.
Exchanges: 1 starch, 3 lean meat,
2 vegetable, 3½ fat

Beef & Onion Fajitas

Spanish Rice
Strawberry Margarita Pie,
page 147

Pork

Mornay-sauced Ham in Pastry Shells

- 1 pkg. (10 oz.) frozen puff pastry shells
- 1 cup frozen peas
- 3 tablespoons margarine or butter
- 3 tablespoons all-purpose flour
- ¼ teaspoon dried thyme leaves
- 1½ cups milk
- 2 cups cubed fully cooked ham (½-inch cubes)
- ½ cup shredded Swiss cheese

6 servings

Prepare pastry shells as directed on package. Set aside. Place peas in 1-quart casserole. Cover. Microwave at High for 4 to 5 minutes, or until tender. Drain. Set aside.

In 8-cup measure, microwave margarine at High for 1 to 1¼ minutes, or until melted. Stir in flour and thyme. Blend in milk. Microwave at High for 4 to 7 minutes, or until mixture thickens and bubbles, stirring twice.

Add ham and peas. Mix well. Microwave at High for 2 to 4 minutes, or until hot. Add cheese, stirring until melted. Spoon ham mixture into pastry shells.

Per Serving: Calories: 415 • Protein: 19 g. • Carbohydrate: 27 g. • Fat: 25 g. • Cholesterol: 38 mg. • Sodium: 933 mg. Exchanges: 1½ starch, 2 lean meat, 4 fat

Mornay-sauced Ham in Pastry Shells

Mixed Green Salad
Fresh Berries

Super-easy Spaghetti

  8 oz. uncooked spaghetti
  1 pkg. (16 oz.) frozen
       cauliflower, broccoli,
       zucchini and carrots
  ¼ cup water
  1 jar (15¼ oz.) spaghetti
       sauce
1½ cups prosciutto ham strips,
       2 × ¼-inch (about 8 oz.)

4 servings

Prepare spaghetti as directed on package. Rinse and drain. Set aside.

In 2-quart casserole, combine vegetables and water. Cover. Micro-wave at High for 6 to 8 minutes, or until vegetables are hot, stirring once. Drain. Add spaghetti sauce and ham strips. Mix well. Re-cover. Microwave at High for 8 to 10 minutes, or until sauce is hot, stirring once. Serve over spaghetti.

Per Serving: Calories: 399 • Protein: 19 g. • Carbohydrate: 68 g. • Fat: 5 g. • Cholesterol: 19 mg. • Sodium: 1188 mg.
Exchanges: 3 starch, ½ lean meat, 4 vegetable, ½ fat

Super-easy Spaghetti

Tossed Salad   *French Bread*

Citrus-sauced Ham Steak

1 lb. fully cooked ham steak,
     about ½ inch thick
½ cup orange juice
⅓ cup honey
¼ cup lemon juice
1 tablespoon plus 1 teaspoon
     cornstarch
½ teaspoon grated orange peel
½ teaspoon grated lemon peel
¼ teaspoon grated lime peel

4 servings

Place ham steak in 10-inch square casserole. Set aside. In 4-cup measure, combine remaining ingredients. Microwave at High for 3 to 5 minutes, or until sauce is thickened and translucent, stirring once. Pour over ham steak. Cover. Microwave at High for 4 to 5 minutes, or until ham is hot.

Per Serving: Calories: 278 • Protein: 24 g. • Carbohydrate: 32 g. • Fat: 6 g.
• Cholesterol: 60 mg. • Sodium: 1367 mg.
Exchanges: 3½ lean meat, 2 fruit

Citrus-sauced Ham Steak
_____

Buttered Broccoli Spears
Baked Potatoes   Chocolate Cake

Apple-Cinnamon Pork Chops

4   pork loin chops (5 to 6 oz.
     each), about ¾ inch thick
1   large apple, cut into ¼-inch
     slices
¼   cup raisins
1   tablespoon cornstarch
1   tablespoon packed brown
     sugar
¼   teaspoon salt
¼   teaspoon ground cinnamon
½   cup apple juice

4 servings

Arrange pork chops in 8-inch square baking dish. Arrange apple slices evenly over chops. Sprinkle with raisins.

In small mixing bowl, combine remaining ingredients. Pour over pork chops. Cover with wax paper or microwave cooking paper. Micro-wave at 70% (Medium High) for 14 to 18 minutes, or until pork is ten-der and no longer pink near bone, stirring sauce mixture once. Let stand, covered, for 5 minutes.

Per Serving: Calories: 364 • Protein: 32 g. • Carbohydrate: 22 g. • Fat: 16 g. • Cholesterol: 89 mg. • Sodium: 189 mg.
Exchanges: 4½ lean meat, 1½ fruit, ½ fat

Apple-Cinnamon Pork Chops

Mixed Vegetables   *Cloverleaf Rolls*

Garden-fresh Pasta Salad

8 oz. uncooked bow tie pasta
   (3 cups)
1 pkg. (16 oz.) frozen broccoli,
   cauliflower and carrots
4 oz. hot pepper Monterey Jack
   cheese, cut into ½-inch
   cubes (¾ cup)
4 oz. hard salami, cut into thin
   strips (1 cup)
½ cup sliced black olives
¼ cup ranch dressing
¼ teaspoon pepper

4 servings

Prepare pasta as directed on package. Rinse and drain. Set aside.

Place vegetables in 3-quart casserole. Cover. Microwave at High for 4 to 7 minutes, or until defrosted, stirring once. Drain.

Add pasta and remaining ingredients. Toss to coat. Serve immediately or cover and chill.

Per Serving: Calories: 494 • Protein: 22 g.
• Carbohydrate: 51 g. • Fat: 23 g.
• Cholesterol: 44 mg. • Sodium: 762 mg.
Exchanges: 3 starch, 1½ high-fat meat,
1 vegetable, 2 fat

Garden-fresh Pasta Salad

Crusty French Bread
Sorbet

Dijon Potato
& Bratwurst Salad

12 oz. new potatoes, cut into
 quarters (about 2 cups)
1½ cups julienne carrots (2 × ¼-
 inch strips)
¼ cup water
1 lb. fully cooked bratwurst,
 diagonally cut into 1 to
 1½-inch pieces
⅓ cup sour cream
2 tablespoons mayonnaise
1 tablespoon Dijon mustard
¼ teaspoon onion powder
¼ teaspoon dried dill weed

6 servings

In 2-quart casserole, combine
potatoes, carrots and water. Cover.
Microwave at High for 8 to 12 minutes, or until tender-crisp, stirring
once. Drain. Add bratwurst. Mix
well. Re-cover. Microwave at High
for 2 to 5 minutes, or until bratwurst
is hot. In small mixing bowl, combine remaining ingredients. Add
to bratwurst mixture. Toss to coat.
Serve warm.

Per Serving: Calories: 351 • Protein: 13 g.
• Carbohydrate: 16 g. • Fat: 26 g.
• Cholesterol: 54 mg. • Sodium: 543 mg.
Exchanges: 1½ starch, 1 high-fat meat,
2 vegetable, 3½ fat

Dijon Potato & Bratwurst Salad

Garlic Toast
Dill Pickle Spears
Assorted Bars

Bacon Corn Chowder

8 slices bacon, cut into 1-inch
   pieces
2 cans (15 oz. each) cream-
   style corn
½ cup milk
1 tablespoon freeze-dried
   chives
¼ teaspoon pepper

6 servings

Place bacon in 2-quart casserole. Cover with paper towel or micro-wave cooking paper. Microwave bacon at High for 4 to 8 minutes, or until brown and crisp, stirring once to break apart. Drain.

Add remaining ingredients. Mix well. Cover. Microwave at High for 6 to 8 minutes, or until hot, stirring once. Top with croutons or cheese popcorn, if desired.

Per Serving: Calories: 161 • Protein: 6 g. • Carbohydrate: 27 g. • Fat: 5 g. • Cholesterol: 9 mg. • Sodium: 548 mg.
Exchanges: 1½ starch, 1 fat

Bacon Corn Chowder

Hard Rolls　　*Cheese Slices*　　*Relishes*

Glazed Smoked Sausage

1   lb. fully cooked smoked
    sausage links
¼   cup chopped green pepper
¼   cup chopped carrot
¼   cup chopped celery
½   cup barbecue sauce

4 to 6 servings

Slice sausages in half lengthwise, leaving one side of skin uncut. Open and place cut-side-up in 10-inch square casserole. Set aside.

Combine vegetables in 1-quart casserole. Cover. Microwave at High for 2 to 4 minutes, or until tender. Add barbecue sauce. Mix well. Spoon evenly over sausages. Cover. Microwave at High for 3 to 5 minutes, or until hot.

Per Serving: Calories: 256 • Protein: 11 g. • Carbohydrate: 6 g. • Fat: 21 g. • Cholesterol: 51 mg. • Sodium: 1032 mg.
Exchanges: 1½ high-fat meat, 1 vegetable, 2 fat

Glazed Smoked Sausage

Deli Coleslaw   *Texas Toast*

Turkey, Spinach
& Strawberry Salad

Chicken

◄ Chicken Mexicana

2½ to 3-lb. broiler-fryer chicken, cut into 8 pieces, skin removed
½ pkg. (1.25 oz.) taco seasoning mix

4 servings

In large plastic food-storage bag, place chicken and taco seasoning mix. Secure bag. Shake to coat.

Arrange chicken pieces in 10-inch square casserole with meaty portions toward outside. Cover with wax paper or microwave cooking paper.

Microwave at High for 13 to 23 minutes, or until meat near bone is no longer pink and juices run clear, rearranging twice. Serve with salsa and sour cream, if desired.

Per Serving: Calories: 178 • Protein: 27 g. • Carbohydrate: 1 g. • Fat: 7 g. • Cholesterol: 81 mg. • Sodium: 189 mg. Exchanges: 3½ lean meat

Chicken Mexicana

Lettuce Salad with Avocado, Oranges & Red Onion Rice Corn on the Cob

Cajun Chicken

2 cups crisp rice cereal, crushed
1½ teaspoons Cajun seasoning
¼ cup margarine or butter
2½ to 3-lb. broiler-fryer chicken, cut into 8 pieces, skin removed

4 servings

In 1-quart casserole, combine cereal and Cajun seasoning. Set aside. In 9-inch pie plate, microwave margarine at High for 1¼ to 1½ minutes, or until melted. Dip chicken pieces in melted margarine. Dredge each piece evenly in cereal mixture, pressing lightly to coat both sides.

In 10-inch square casserole, arrange chicken pieces with meaty portions toward outside. Cover with wax paper or microwave cooking paper. Microwave at High for 13 to 23 minutes, or until meat near bone is no longer pink and juices run clear, rearranging twice. Serve with salsa, if desired.

Per Serving: Calories: 371 • Protein: 33 g. • Carbohydrate: 14 g. • Fat: 20 g. • Cholesterol: 97 mg. • Sodium: 354 mg. Exchanges: 1 starch, 4 lean mean, 1½ fat

Cajun Chicken

Buttermilk Biscuits Deli Coleslaw or Potato Salad Butter Pecan Ice Cream

Chicken with Sour Cream Basil Sauce

2 bone-in whole chicken breasts (10 to 12 oz. each), split in half, skin removed
¼ cup orange juice, divided
¾ teaspoon dried basil leaves, divided
⅛ teaspoon pepper
½ cup sour cream
½ teaspoon sugar
⅛ teaspoon salt

4 servings

In 10-inch square casserole, arrange chicken breast halves with meaty portions toward outside.

In small bowl, combine 2 tablespoons orange juice, ½ teaspoon basil and the pepper. Sprinkle over chicken. Cover. Microwave at High for 11 to 14 minutes, or until meat near bone is no longer pink and juices run clear, rotating and basting chicken with liquid in casserole once. Let stand, covered, for 3 minutes.

In small mixing bowl, combine the remaining 2 tablespoons orange juice and ¼ teaspoon basil, the sour cream, sugar and salt. Serve sauce over chicken.

Per Serving: Calories: 305 • Protein: 35 g. • Carbohydrate: 17 g. • Fat: 10 g. • Cholesterol: 104 mg. • Sodium: 163 mg. Exchanges: 4 lean meat, 1 fruit, 1 fat

Chicken with Sour Cream Basil Sauce

Tomato & Cucumber Salad Frozen Fruit Yogurt

Herb-crumbed Chicken Breasts

1 cup buttery cracker crumbs (about 24 crackers)
1 teaspoon dried marjoram leaves
1 teaspoon dried parsley flakes
1 teaspoon onion salt
3 tablespoons margarine or butter
2 bone-in whole chicken breasts (10 to 12 oz. each), split in half, skin removed

4 servings

In 1-quart casserole, combine cracker crumbs, marjoram, parsley and onion salt. Set aside.

In 9-inch pie plate, microwave margarine at High for 1 to 1¼ minutes, or until melted. Dip chicken in melted margarine. Dredge each piece evenly in crumb mixture, pressing lightly to coat both sides.

Arrange chicken breasts in 11 × 7-inch baking dish with meaty portions toward outside. Cover with wax paper or microwave cooking paper. Microwave at High for 12 to 15 minutes, or until meat near bone is no longer pink and juices run clear, rearranging twice.

Per Serving: Calories: 334 • Protein: 34 g. • Carbohydrate: 12 g. • Fat: 15 g. • Cholesterol: 90 mg. • Sodium: 776 mg. Exchanges: 1 starch, 4 lean meat, 1 fat

Herb-crumbed Chicken Breasts

New Potatoes
Green Beans
Chocolate Pudding

Creamy Thyme Chicken

2 boneless whole chicken breasts (8 to 10 oz. each), split in half, skin removed
¼ teaspoon onion powder
1 pkg. (0.87 oz.) white sauce mix
¼ teaspoon dried thyme leaves
1 cup milk
1 jar (4.5 oz.) sliced mushrooms, drained

4 servings

Arrange chicken breasts in 10-inch square casserole with meaty portions toward outside. Sprinkle evenly with onion powder. Cover with wax paper or microwave cooking paper. Microwave at High for 6 to 9 minutes, or until meat is no longer pink and juices run clear, rearranging once. Drain. Set aside.

In 2-cup measure, combine white sauce mix and thyme. Blend in milk with whisk. Microwave at High for 4½ to 6 minutes, or until sauce thickens and bubbles, stirring twice. Add mushrooms. Mix well. Pour sauce over chicken. Re-cover. Microwave at High for 2 to 3 minutes, or until hot.

Per Serving: Calories: 207 • Protein: 30 g.
• Carbohydrate: 8 g. • Fat: 6 g.
• Cholesterol: 77 mg. • Sodium: 424 mg.
Exchanges: 3½ lean meat, ½ vegetable, ½ low-fat milk

Creamy Thyme Chicken

Green Beans with Almonds
Strawberry Jello Salad

Chicken Mozzarella ▲

4 frozen fully cooked breaded chicken patties
4 thin slices tomato
½ cup spaghetti sauce
1 cup shredded mozzarella cheese
2 tablespoons snipped fresh parsley

4 servings

Place frozen chicken patties on paper towel in 10-inch square casserole. Microwave at High for 5 to 6 minutes, or until hot, turning over once. Remove paper towel, leaving patties in casserole.

Top each patty with tomato slice. Spoon 2 tablespoons spaghetti sauce over each patty. Sprinkle each evenly with cheese and parsley. Microwave at 70% (Medium High) for 2 to 3 minutes, or until patties are hot and cheese is melted.

Per Serving: Calories: 340 • Protein: 21 g. • Carbohydrate: 19 g. • Fat: 20 g.
• Cholesterol: 15 mg. • Sodium: 818 mg.
Exchanges: 1 starch, 2½ medium-fat meat, 1 vegetable, 1½ fat

Chicken Mozzarella

Romaine with Red Onion Salad
Ice Cream with Chocolate Sauce

Ranch Chicken Star Sandwich

1 boneless whole chicken breast (8 to 10 oz.), skin removed, cut into ½-inch pieces
½ cup seeded chopped cucumber
½ cup seeded chopped tomato
¼ cup ranch dressing
4 pitas (4-inch)
¼ cup alfalfa sprouts
¼ cup shredded Cheddar cheese

4 servings

Per Serving: Calories: 236 • Protein: 18 g. • Carbohydrate: 14 g. • Fat: 13 g. • Cholesterol: 44 mg. • Sodium: 278 mg. Exchanges: 1 starch, 2 lean meat, 1 fat

Ranch Chicken Star Sandwich

Carrot & Celery Sticks
Dill Pickle Spears
Fresh Fruit
Sparkling Water

How to Microwave Ranch Chicken Star Sandwich

Place chicken in 1-quart casserole. Cover. Microwave at High for 2 to 3 minutes, or until meat is no longer pink, stirring once. Drain. In medium mixing bowl, combine chicken, cucumber, tomato and dressing. Set aside.

Cut a cross through top layer of each pita, cutting to outer edge of circle. Open carefully. Spoon about ½ cup chicken mixture into each pita. Top each with 1 tablespoon alfalfa sprouts and 1 tablespoon cheese.

Place filled sandwiches on paper-towel-lined plate. Microwave at 70% (Medium High) for 2½ to 3 minutes, or until cheese is melted, rotating plate once.

Cheesy Chicken Tacos

1 pkg. (16 oz.) frozen
   vegetables and pasta with
   garlic seasoning
2 cans (5 oz. each) chunk
   white chicken, drained
½ cup cubed pasteurized
   process cheese loaf with
   jalapeño pepper (½-inch
   cubes)
¼ cup water
½ teaspoon chili powder
8 taco shells
½ cup seeded chopped tomato
¼ cup sliced green onions

4 servings

In 2-quart casserole, combine
vegetable and pasta mixture,
chicken, cheese, water and chili
powder. Cover. Microwave at High
for 10 to 13 minutes, or until mixture is hot and cheese is melted,
stirring 3 times. Spoon mixture
evenly into taco shells.

Arrange taco shells upright in
11 × 7-inch baking dish. Microwave at High for 3 to 4 minutes,
or until hot, rotating dish once.
Sprinkle with tomato and onions.
Serve with salsa, if desired.

Per Serving: Calories: 385 • Protein: 25 g.
• Carbohydrate: 37 g. • Fat: 17 g. •
Cholesterol: 72 mg. • Sodium: 1009 mg.
Exchanges: 2 starch, 2 lean meat,
1½ vegetable, 2 fat

Cheesy Chicken Tacos

Melon Wedges

Rosemary Chicken & Vegetables ▲

  2 boneless whole chicken breasts (8 to 10 oz. each), skin removed, cut into 1-inch pieces
  1 lb. new potatoes, quartered (about 8 potatoes)
1½ cups frozen cut green beans
  2 tablespoons olive oil
  2 teaspoons lemon juice
 ½ teaspoon salt
 ½ teaspoon sugar
 ½ teaspoon dried rosemary leaves, crushed
 ⅛ teaspoon garlic powder

4 servings

In 10-inch square casserole, combine chicken, potatoes and green beans. In small bowl, combine remaining ingredients. Add to chicken mixture. Mix well. Cover. Microwave at High for 14 to 18 minutes, or until meat is no longer pink, juices run clear and potatoes are tender, stirring twice.

Per Serving: Calories: 308 • Protein: 30 g. • Carbohydrate: 25 g. • Fat: 10 g. • Cholesterol: 72 mg. • Sodium: 338 mg.
Exchanges: 1 starch, 3 lean meat, 2 vegetable

Rosemary Chicken & Vegetables

Sliced Watermelon
Iced Tea

Creamed Chicken & Biscuits

  1 pkg. (7½ oz.) refrigerated buttermilk biscuits
  1 pkg. (1.8 oz.) white sauce mix
  2 cups milk
  2 cups frozen mixed vegetables
  2 cans (5 oz. each) chunk white chicken, drained

5 servings

Prepare biscuits as directed on package. Set aside. Place white sauce mix in 4-cup measure. Blend in milk with whisk. Microwave at High for 6 to 10 minutes, or until white sauce thickens and bubbles, stirring twice.

Add vegetables and chicken. Mix well. Cover with plastic wrap. Microwave at High for 2 to 3 minutes, or until hot, stirring once. Place 2 biscuits on each plate. Spoon about ¾ cup chicken mixture over each serving.

Per Serving: Calories: 312 • Protein: 22 g. • Carbohydrate: 37 g. • Fat: 9 g. • Cholesterol: 47 mg. • Sodium: 988 mg.
Exchanges: 1½ starch, 1½ lean meat, 2 vegetable, ½ low-fat milk

Creamed Chicken & Biscuits

Mixed Green Salad
Peach Slices & Oatmeal Cookies

Crunchy Cheddar Chicken Casserole ▲

1 pkg. (16 oz.) frozen vegetables and pasta with creamy Cheddar seasoning
2 cans (5 oz. each) chunk white chicken, drained
1 cup cubed pasteurized process cheese loaf (½-inch cubes)
¼ cup water
1 cup onion-and-garlic-seasoned croutons

4 servings

In 2-quart casserole, combine all ingredients except croutons. Cover. Microwave at High for 10 to 13 minutes, or until mixture is hot and cheese is melted, stirring 3 times. Add croutons. Mix well. Serve immediately.

Per Serving: Calories: 371 • Protein: 28 g. • Carbohydrate: 27 g. • Fat: 17 g. • Cholesterol: 77 mg. • Sodium: 1189 mg.
Exchanges: 1 starch, 2½ lean meat, 2½ vegetable, 2 fat

Crunchy Cheddar Chicken Casserole

Bread Sticks
Fresh Fruit in Vanilla Yogurt

Almond Couscous Chicken Salad

⅓ cup mayonnaise
1 tablespoon soy sauce
1 teaspoon sugar
¼ teaspoon ground ginger
1¼ cups hot water
¾ cup uncooked couscous
2 cans (5 oz. each) chunk white chicken, drained
¼ cup slivered almonds
1 can (11 oz.) mandarin orange segments, drained

4 to 6 servings

In small mixing bowl, combine mayonnaise, soy sauce, sugar and ginger. Set aside. Place water in 2-quart casserole. Cover. Microwave at High for 4 to 6 minutes, or until boiling. Add couscous. Mix well. Let stand, covered, for 5 minutes.

Add mayonnaise mixture, chicken and almonds to couscous. Mix well. Gently fold in oranges. Serve immediately or refrigerate and serve cold.

Per Serving: Calories: 287 • Protein: 15 g. • Carbohydrate: 22 g. • Fat: 16 g. • Cholesterol: 40 mg. • Sodium: 431 mg.
Exchanges: 1 starch, 1½ lean meat, ½ fruit, 2 fat

Almond Couscous Chicken Salad

Iced Tea

Creamy Chicken & Mostaccioli

8 oz. uncooked mostaccioli
2 boneless whole chicken breasts (8 to 10 oz. each), skin removed, cut into 1-inch pieces
½ cup chopped green pepper
1 can (10¾ oz.) condensed cream of mushroom soup
½ cup milk
1 jar (2 oz.) diced pimiento, drained
¼ teaspoon onion powder
2 tablespoons shredded fresh Parmesan cheese

6 servings

Prepare mostaccioli as directed on package. Rinse and drain. Set aside.

In 3-quart casserole, place chicken and pepper. Cover. Microwave at High for 4 to 6½ minutes, or until meat is no longer pink, stirring twice. Drain. Set aside.

In small mixing bowl, combine soup, milk, pimiento and onion powder. Add soup mixture and mostaccioli to chicken. Mix well. Re-cover. Microwave at High for 4 to 6 minutes, or until hot, stirring once. Sprinkle with cheese.

Per Serving: Calories: 310 • Protein: 25 g.
• Carbohydrate: 34 g. • Fat: 7 g. •
Cholesterol: 52 mg. • Sodium: 504 mg.
Exchanges: 2 starch, 2½ lean meat,
1 vegetable

Creamy Chicken & Mostaccioli

Crisp Vegetable Sticks
Popovers

Chicken Potato Chowder

1 boneless whole chicken breast (8 to 10 oz.), skin removed, cut into ½-inch pieces
½ cup finely chopped onion
2 cups frozen broccoli cuts
1½ cups milk
1 can (10¾ oz.) condensed cream of potato soup
¼ teaspoon dried basil leaves
Dash pepper
½ cup shredded Swiss cheese

4 servings

In 3-quart casserole, combine chicken and onion. Cover. Microwave at High for 2½ to 3 minutes, or until meat is no longer pink and juices run clear, stirring once.

Add remaining ingredients, except cheese. Mix well. Re-cover. Microwave at High for 8 to 10 minutes, or until broccoli is tender, stirring once or twice. Stir in cheese.

Let stand, covered, for 5 minutes, or until cheese is melted.

Per Serving: Calories: 236 • Protein: 23 g. • Carbohydrate: 16 g. • Fat: 9 g. • Cholesterol: 60 mg. • Sodium: 736 mg. Exchanges: ½ starch, 2½ lean meat, 2 vegetable

Chicken Potato Chowder

Dark Rye Bread
Red or Green Grapes

Country Chicken Soup ▲

2 cups hot water
2 cups frozen mixed vegetables
1 can (14½ oz.) ready-to-serve chicken broth
1 can (5 oz.) chunk white chicken, drained
½ cup uncooked alphabet macaroni
¼ teaspoon dried thyme leaves
¼ teaspoon salt
Dash pepper

4 servings

In 3-quart casserole, combine all ingredients. Cover. Microwave at High for 21 to 26 minutes, or until macaroni is tender, stirring once or twice.

Per Serving: Calories: 131 • Protein: 13 g. • Carbohydrate: 15 g. • Fat: 2 g. • Cholesterol: 24 mg. • Sodium: 614 mg.
Exchanges: 1 starch, 1 lean meat

Country Chicken Soup

Sourdough Bread
Apple & Cheddar Cheese Slices

Turkey

◄ Savory Turkey & Corn

1 pkg. (12 oz.) frozen corn soufflé
½ cup herb-seasoned stuffing mix
¼ cup sliced green onions
1 jar (2 oz.) diced pimiento, drained
2 turkey tenderloins (8 to 10 oz. each)
1 tablespoon margarine or butter
⅛ teaspoon dried rubbed sage leaves
⅛ teaspoon paprika

4 to 6 servings

Remove corn soufflé from packaging. Place in medium mixing bowl. Microwave at High for 3 to 4 minutes, or until defrosted. Add stuffing mix, onions and pimiento. Mix well. Spread corn mixture evenly in bottom of 8-inch square baking dish. Arrange turkey tenderloins over corn mixture with meaty portions toward outside. Set aside.

In small bowl, microwave margarine, sage and paprika at High for 30 to 45 seconds, or until margarine is melted. Brush each tenderloin with margarine mixture. Cover with wax paper or microwave cooking paper. Microwave at 70% (Medium High) for 15 to 25 minutes, or until meat is no longer pink and juices run clear, rotating dish twice. Let stand, covered, for 3 minutes.

Per Serving: Calories: 220 • Protein: 25 g. • Carbohydrate: 14 g.
• Fat: 6 g. • Cholesterol: 60 mg. • Sodium: 430 mg.
Exchanges: 1 starch, 3 lean meat

Savory Turkey & Corn

Buttered Zucchini
Bosc Pears

Turkey, Spinach & Strawberry Salad

1 turkey tenderloin (8 to 10 oz.)
¼ teaspoon seasoned salt
8 cups torn fresh spinach leaves
2 cups sliced strawberries

Dressing:
⅓ cup mayonnaise
¼ cup milk
2 teaspoons sugar
2 teaspoons Dijon mustard
1 teaspoon prepared mustard
¼ cup sliced green onions

4 servings

Place turkey tenderloin in 9-inch pie plate. Sprinkle evenly with seasoned salt. Cover with plastic wrap. Microwave at 70% (Medium High) for 12 to 15 minutes, or until meat is no longer pink and juices run clear, rotating dish twice. Let stand for 5 minutes.

Arrange spinach and strawberries evenly on 4 plates. Slice tenderloin thinly, to yield 12 slices. Arrange 3 slices on each salad.

In small mixing bowl, combine all dressing ingredients, except green onions. Mix well with whisk. Spoon about 2 tablespoons dressing over each salad. Sprinkle evenly with green onions.

Per Serving: Calories: 275 • Protein: 18 g. • Carbohydrate: 17 g.
• Fat: 17 g. • Cholesterol: 47 mg. • Sodium: 412 mg.
Exchanges: 2 lean meat, 1 vegetable, 1 fruit, 2 fat

Turkey, Spinach & Strawberry Salad

Lemonade   *Sugar Cookies*

Turkey Slices with Fruit Salsa

1 tablespoon packed brown
   sugar
1 tablespoon cornstarch
¼ teaspoon ground cinnamon
1 can (8 oz.) pineapple tidbits
   in juice, drained (reserve
   juice)
¼ cup raisins
1 medium orange, peeled and
   chopped
1 lb. uncooked turkey breast
   slices

4 servings

In 2-cup measure, combine brown sugar, cornstarch and cinnamon.
Add reserved pineapple juice plus water to equal ½ cup. Mix well.
Add raisins. Mix well. Microwave at High for 1½ to 3 minutes, or until
mixture is thickened and translucent, stirring once. Add pineapple
and orange. Mix well. Set aside.

Arrange turkey slices in 10-inch square casserole. Cover. Microwave
at 70% (Medium High) for 7 to 10 minutes, or until meat is no longer
pink and juices run clear, turning and rearranging slices once. Spoon
fruit mixture over turkey. Re-cover. Microwave at High for 4 to 5 minutes, or until hot.

Per Serving: Calories: 212 • Protein: 26 g. • Carbohydrate: 25 g. • Fat: 1 g.
• Cholesterol: 71 mg. • Sodium: 47 mg.
Exchanges: 3 lean meat, 1½ fruit

Turkey Slices with Fruit Salsa

Brown Rice   Tossed Green Salad

Wild Rice Turkey Bake ▶

1½ cups cooked wild rice
    (½ cup uncooked)
8 oz. fully cooked turkey,
    sliced
3 tablespoons margarine
    or butter
3 tablespoons all-purpose
    flour
½ teaspoon salt
¼ teaspoon dried tarragon
    leaves
1½ cups milk
2 cups frozen broccoli,
    cauliflower and carrots

4 servings

Spoon wild rice evenly into 8-inch square baking dish. Top with turkey slices. Set aside.

In 4-cup measure, microwave margarine at High for 1 to 1¼ minutes, or until melted. Stir in flour, salt and tarragon. Blend in milk with whisk. Microwave at High for 4 to 6½ minutes, or until mixture thickens and bubbles, stirring twice. Add frozen vegetables. Mix well.

Microwave at High for 2 to 3 minutes, or until vegetables are defrosted. Spoon over turkey and rice. Cover with wax paper or microwave cooking paper. Microwave at High for 5 to 6 minutes, or until hot, rotating dish once.

Per Serving: Calories: 402 • Protein: 28 g. • Carbohydrate: 43 g. • Fat: 14 g. • Cholesterol: 50 mg. • Sodium: 476 mg. Exchanges: 2 starch, 2 lean meat, 1½ vegetable, ½ low-fat milk, 1 fat

Wild Rice Turkey Bake

Dinner Rolls
Fresh Fruit Compote

Easy Turkey & Stuffing Supper

1 pkg. (6 oz.) chicken-flavored
    stuffing mix (2½ cups
    prepared stuffing)
8 oz. fully cooked turkey, sliced

1 can (18 oz.) sweet potatoes,
    drained
½ cup sour cream
·2 tablespoons sliced green
    onion

4 servings

Prepare stuffing as directed on package. Arrange turkey in 8-inch square baking dish. Spoon stuffing evenly over turkey. Top with sweet potatoes. Cover with plastic wrap. Microwave at 70% (Medium High) for 5 to 8 minutes, or until hot, rotating dish twice. Spoon sour cream evenly over sweet potatoes. Sprinkle with onions. Re-cover. Microwave at 70% (Medium High) for 5 to 6 minutes, or until onions are tender-crisp, rotating dish once.

Per Serving: Calories: 408 • Protein: 24 g. • Carbohydrate: 53 g. • Fat: 11 g. • Cholesterol: 58 mg. • Sodium: 654 mg. Exchanges: 3½ starch, 2 lean meat, 1 fat

Easy Turkey & Stuffing Supper

Green Beans
Pecan Apple Crumble, page 153

Teriyaki Turkey Patties

- 1 lb. ground turkey
- 2 tablespoons unseasoned dry bread crumbs
- ¼ cup soy sauce, divided
- 1 cup julienne carrots (2 × ¼-inch strips)
- 1 cup sliced celery
- 3 tablespoons packed brown sugar
- 1 tablespoon plus 1 teaspoon cornstarch
- ¼ teaspoon ground ginger
- ¼ cup water

4 servings

In small mixing bowl, combine ground turkey, bread crumbs and 2 tablespoons soy sauce. Mix well. Shape mixture into four 4-inch round patties. Arrange patties in 10-inch square casserole. Top with carrots and celery. Set aside.

In small mixing bowl, combine brown sugar, cornstarch and ginger. Blend in the remaining 2 tablespoons soy sauce and the water. Pour over turkey patties and vegetables. Cover. Microwave at High for 12 to 22 minutes, or until patties are firm, rearranging and basting with sauce twice.

Per Serving: Calories: 247 • Protein: 25 g. • Carbohydrate: 20 g. • Fat: 8 g. • Cholesterol: 76 mg. • Sodium: 1167 mg. Exchanges: ½ starch, 3 lean meat, 2 vegetable

Turkey Chow Mein ▲

- 1 cup julienne carrots (2 × ¼-inch strips)
- 1 cup diagonally sliced celery (½-inch slices)
- 1 tablespoon packed brown sugar
- 2 tablespoons cornstarch
- 1¼ cups ready-to-serve chicken broth
- 1 tablespoon soy sauce
- 1½ cups fully cooked turkey, cut into ½-inch pieces
- 1 cup bean sprouts
- ¼ cup sliced green onions

4 servings

In 2-quart casserole, place carrots and celery. Add brown sugar and cornstarch. Blend in chicken broth and soy sauce. Mix well. Cover.

Microwave at High for 6 to 8 minutes, or until sauce is thickened and translucent and vegetables are tender, stirring 2 or 3 times.

Add turkey, sprouts and onions. Mix well. Microwave at High for 2 to 3 minutes, or until hot. Serve over hot cooked rice or chow mein noodles, if desired.

Per Serving: Calories: 150 • Protein: 18 g. • Carbohydrate: 11 g. • Fat: 3 g. • Cholesterol: 40 mg. • Sodium: 576 mg. Exchanges: 2 lean meat, 2 vegetable

Turkey Chow Mein

*Sherry Marmalade Oranges, page 152
Fortune Cookies*

Teriyaki Turkey Patties

*Steamed Rice
Orange Sherbet*

Italian-style Turkey Meatballs

8 oz. uncooked spaghetti
½ lb. ground turkey
¼ cup grated Parmesan cheese
1 can (15 oz.) tomato sauce
1 jar (4.5 oz.) sliced
   mushrooms, drained
½ cup sliced green pepper
¼ cup chopped onion
¼ teaspoon dried basil leaves
¼ teaspoon dried oregano
   leaves

4 servings

Prepare spaghetti as directed on package. Rinse and drain. Set aside.

In medium mixing bowl, combine turkey and cheese. Shape into 12 to 14 meatballs, about 1 inch in diameter. Arrange meatballs around outer edge of 10-inch pie plate. Cover with wax paper or microwave cooking paper. Microwave at High for 4 to 5½ minutes, or until meatballs are firm and no longer pink, rearranging twice. Drain. Set aside.

In 2-quart casserole, combine remaining ingredients. Cover. Microwave at High for 3 to 4 minutes, or until sauce is hot and green pepper is tender-crisp.

Add meatballs. Mix well. Cover. Microwave at High for 3 to 4 minutes, or until hot, stirring once. Serve over spaghetti. Sprinkle with additional grated Parmesan cheese, if desired.

Per Serving: Calories: 361 • Protein: 23 g. • Carbohydrate: 53 g. • Fat: 7 g.
• Cholesterol: 43 mg. • Sodium: 918 mg.
Exchanges: 2 starch, 1½ lean meat, 4½ vegetable

Italian-style Turkey Meatballs

Crusty French Bread   *Mixed Greens with Croutons*

Super-quick Fish & Seafood

Fish Olé

Fish

◄ Dilly Cod Salad

2 tablespoons margarine or butter
½ teaspoon dried dill weed, divided
½ teaspoon lemon pepper, divided
1 pkg. (8 oz.) frozen cod fillets
1 cup seeded chopped tomato
1 cup sliced cucumber
½ cup sliced celery
¼ cup sliced green onions
½ cup plain low-fat yogurt
½ cup mayonnaise

4 servings

In 11 × 7-inch baking dish, microwave margarine at High for 45 seconds to 1 minute, or until melted. Add ¼ teaspoon dill weed and ¼ teaspoon lemon pepper. Mix well.

Dip each frozen fillet in margarine mixture to coat. Arrange in baking dish. Cover with wax paper or microwave cooking paper. Microwave at High for 4½ to 6½ minutes, or until fish flakes easily with fork, rearranging once. Cut fish into ¾-inch cubes.

In large mixing bowl or salad bowl, combine fish, tomato, cucumber, celery and onions. Set aside. In small mixing bowl, combine yogurt, mayonnaise and remaining ¼ teaspoon dill weed and lemon pepper. Arrange salad on 4 lettuce-lined plates. Top evenly with dressing.

Per Serving: Calories: 335 • Protein: 13 g. • Carbohydrate: 7 g.
• Fat: 29 g. • Cholesterol: 43 mg. • Sodium: 373 mg.
Exchanges: 1½ lean meat, 1½ vegetable, 4½ fat

Dilly Cod Salad

Crescent Rolls

Crunchy Salmon Patties

2 cans (6½ oz. each) skinless, boneless salmon, drained
1½ cups cornflake crumbs, divided
½ cup mayonnaise
1 egg
2 tablespoons sliced green onion
½ teaspoon prepared mustard

4 servings

In medium mixing bowl, combine salmon, ½ cup cornflake crumbs, the mayonnaise, egg, onion and mustard. Shape into 4 patties, about 4 inches in diameter. Place remaining 1 cup cornflake crumbs in 9-inch pie plate. Dredge each patty evenly in cornflake crumbs, pressing lightly to coat both sides.

Arrange patties in 10-inch square casserole. Cover with wax paper or microwave cooking paper. Microwave at High for 4½ to 6 minutes, or until firm and hot, rotating casserole once.

Serve salmon patties topped with tartar sauce, if desired.

Per Serving: Calories: 459 • Protein: 20 g. • Carbohydrate: 29 g.
• Fat: 29 g. • Cholesterol: 103 mg. • Sodium: 911 mg.
Exchanges: 2 starch, 2 lean meat, 4 fat

Crunchy Salmon Patties

Asparagus Spears   *Fresh Fruit*

Fresh Sole Divan

- 2 tablespoons margarine or butter
- 2 teaspoons freeze-dried chives
- 4 sole fillets (about 2 oz. each)
- ½ pkg. (16 oz.) frozen broccoli spears
- ½ cup mayonnaise
- 1 teaspoon prepared mustard Paprika

4 servings

In 10-inch square casserole, microwave margarine and chives at High for 45 seconds to 1 minute, or until margarine is melted. Mix well. Dip fillets in margarine mixture to coat. Arrange fillets in casserole. Cover with wax paper or microwave cooking paper. Microwave at High for 3½ to 5 minutes, or until fish flakes easily with fork, rearranging once. Set aside.

Place broccoli spears in 1-quart casserole. Cover. Microwave at High for 4 to 5 minutes, or until broccoli is tender-crisp, stirring once. Drain.

In small mixing bowl, combine mayonnaise and mustard. Spoon sauce evenly over fillets. Arrange 2 or 3 broccoli spears over each fillet. Sprinkle with paprika.

Per Serving: Calories: 338 • Protein: 15 g.
• Carbohydrate: 7 g. • Fat: 29 g. •
Cholesterol: 44 mg. • Sodium: 307 mg.
Exchanges: 2 lean meat, 1½ vegetable,
4½ fat

Fresh Sole Divan

Dinner Rolls
Cherry Peach Cream Pie,
page 145

Mexican-style Fish ▲

　3　tablespoons margarine or butter
　¼　teaspoon garlic powder
　⅛　teaspoon cayenne
　4　sole fillets (3 oz. each)
　⅓　cup shredded Cheddar cheese
　½　cup seeded chopped tomato
　¼　cup sliced green onions

4 servings

In 10-inch square casserole, microwave margarine at High for 1 to 1¼ minutes, or until melted. Add garlic powder and cayenne. Mix well.

Dip fillets in margarine mixture to coat. Arrange fillets in casserole. Cover. Microwave at High for 3½ to 6 minutes, or until fish flakes easily with fork, rearranging once. Sprinkle each fillet evenly with cheese. Spoon tomato and onions over fillets. Serve with dollop of sour cream, if desired.

Per Serving: Calories: 198 • Protein: 19 g. • Carbohydrate: 2 g. • Fat: 13 g. • Cholesterol: 51 mg. • Sodium: 230 mg.
Exchanges: 2½ lean meat, 1 fat

Mexican-style Fish

Mexican Rice
Lime Sherbet　　*Sugar Cookies*

Orange-glazed Orange Roughy

　1　lb. orange roughy fillets
　½　cup orange marmalade
　1　tablespoon soy sauce
　¼　teaspoon garlic powder
　⅛　teaspoon salt

4 servings

Arrange fillets in 10-inch square casserole. In small mixing bowl, combine marmalade, soy sauce, garlic powder and salt. Spoon over fillets. Cover with wax paper or microwave cooking paper. Microwave at High for 5 to 10 minutes, or until fish flakes easily with fork, rearranging once.

Per Serving: Calories: 249 • Protein: 17 g. • Carbohydrate: 29 g. • Fat: 8 g. • Cholesterol: 23 mg. • Sodium: 401 mg.
Exchanges: 2½ lean meat, 2 fruit

Orange-glazed Orange Roughy

Frozen Mixed Vegetables
Rice

Sole & Vegetables with Soy Butter ▲

     3 tablespoons margarine or butter
     2 teaspoons soy sauce
     4 thin sole fillets (3 oz. each)
    ½ cup shredded carrot
    ½ cup julienne zucchini (2 × ¼-inch strips)
    ⅓ cup sliced green onions
        Garlic salt
        Cracked pepper

4 servings

In 11 × 7-inch baking dish, microwave margarine at High for 1 to 1¼ minutes, or until melted. Add soy sauce. Mix well. Dip each fillet in margarine mixture to coat. Arrange fillets in baking dish. Cover with plastic wrap. Microwave at High for 3½ to 6 minutes, or until fish flakes easily with fork, rearranging once. Let stand, covered, for 3 minutes.

In 1-quart casserole, combine carrot, zucchini and onions. Cover. Microwave at High for 1 to 2 minutes, or until vegetables are hot and color brightens. Spoon over fillets. Sprinkle with garlic salt and cracked pepper.

Per Serving: Calories: 166 • Protein: 17 g. • Carbohydrate: 3 g. • Fat: 10 g. • Cholesterol: 41 mg. • Sodium: 376 mg.
Exchanges: 2½ lean meat, ½ vegetable, ½ fat

Sole & Vegetables with Soy Butter

Rice
Lemon Sorbet

Fish Olé

    10 thin sole fillets, 5 to 6 inches long
         (about 2 oz. each)
     3 tablespoons plus 1 teaspoon Mexican-
         flavored cheese spread
     1 can (2.5 oz) sliced black olives, drained
     2 tablespoons margarine or butter
    ¾ cup crushed taco chips (2 cups uncrushed)

4 servings

Spread each fillet with 1 teaspoon cheese. Sprinkle each with 2 teaspoons olives. Roll up each fillet, starting at narrow end. Set aside. In 9-inch pie plate, microwave margarine at High for 45 seconds to 1 minute, or until melted.

Place crushed taco chips in 1-quart casserole. Dip each rolled fillet in margarine. Roll in taco chips, pressing lightly to coat. Arrange rolled fillets around edge of pie plate. Cover with wax paper or microwave cooking paper. Microwave at High for 5 to 7 minutes, or until fish flakes easily with fork, rearranging once. Serve rolled fillets with salsa, if desired.

Per Serving: Calories: 198 • Protein: 14 g. • Carbohydrate: 8 g. • Fat: 12 g. • Cholesterol: 34 mg. • Sodium: 420 mg.
Exchanges: ½ starch, 2 lean meat, 1 fat

Fish Olé

Refried Beans   Mexican Rice
Strawberries Topped with Cream

Tuna Balls
with Cream Sauce

2 cans (6½ oz. each) solid
    white tuna, water pack,
    drained and flaked
2 cups cornflake crumbs,
    divided
⅓ cup mayonnaise
1 egg
2 tablespoons sliced green
    onion
1 teaspoon prepared mustard
1 pkg. (1.8 oz.) white sauce mix
2 cups milk
1 cup frozen peas
¼ teaspoon dried dill weed

4 servings

Per Serving: Calories: 576 • Protein: 37 g.
• Carbohydrate: 55 g. • Fat: 23 g. •
Cholesterol: 89 mg. • Sodium: 1403 mg.
Exchanges: 3 starch, 3 lean meat,
½ low-fat milk, 2½ fat

Tuna Balls with Cream Sauce

Buttered Egg Noodles

How to Microwave Tuna Balls with Cream Sauce

Combine tuna, 1 cup cornflake crumbs, the mayonnaise, egg, onion and mustard in medium mixing bowl. Shape into 12 balls, 1½ inches in diameter. Place remaining 1 cup cornflake crumbs in shallow dish. Roll each ball in crumbs to coat evenly.

Arrange tuna balls in 9-inch pie plate. Cover with wax paper or microwave cooking paper. Microwave at High for 3½ to 6 minutes, or until firm, rearranging once.

Place white sauce mix in 4-cup measure. Blend in milk with whisk. Microwave at High for 6 to 10 minutes, or until sauce thickens and bubbles, stirring every 2 minutes. Add peas and dill weed. Mix well. Microwave at High for 2 to 3 minutes, or until hot, stirring once. Serve over tuna balls.

Tuna Burger Supreme

1 can (6½ oz.) solid white tuna, water pack, drained and flaked
½ cup finely crushed saltine crackers
⅓ cup shredded carrot
⅓ cup chopped celery
⅓ cup salad dressing
2 tablespoons chopped red onion
4 hamburger buns, split
4 tomato slices
⅓ cup shredded Cheddar cheese

4 servings

In medium mixing bowl, combine tuna, cracker crumbs, carrot, celery, dressing and onion. Set aside.

Line 10-inch square casserole with paper towel or microwave cooking paper. Place bottom halves of hamburger buns in casserole. Spoon heaping ⅓ cup tuna mixture evenly over each. Top each burger with tomato slice. Sprinkle each evenly with cheese. Microwave at High for 2 to 2½ minutes, or until tuna burgers are hot and cheese is melted, rotating casserole once. Cover with top halves of buns.

Per Serving: Calories: 357 • Protein: 19 g. • Carbohydrate: 32 g. • Fat: 17 g.
• Cholesterol: 28 mg. • Sodium: 635 mg.
Exchanges: 1½ starch, 1½ lean meat, 2 vegetable, 2½ fat

Tuna Burger Supreme

Potato Chips   *Relishes & Pickles*

Salmon Pasta Salad

2 cups uncooked microwave
    elbow macaroni
1 can (6½ oz.) skinless,
    boneless salmon, drained
1 large apple, cored and
    chopped (about 1¼ cups)
½ cup sliced celery
½ cup coarsely chopped
    walnuts
½ teaspoon onion salt
½ cup mayonnaise
1 tablespoon sugar
2 teaspoons lemon juice

4 to 6 servings

Prepare macaroni as directed on package. Rinse and drain.

In large mixing bowl or salad bowl, combine macaroni, salmon, apple, celery, walnuts and onion salt. Toss to combine.

In small mixing bowl, combine remaining ingredients. Add dressing to salad. Toss to coat. Cover with plastic wrap. Chill at least 2 hours. Arrange salad on lettuce-lined plates, if desired.

Per Serving: Calories: 421 • Protein: 12 g. • Carbohydrate: 42 g. • Fat: 23 g.
• Cholesterol: 22 mg. • Sodium: 384 mg.
Exchanges: 1½ starch, 1 lean meat, 1 vegetable, 1 fruit, 3½ fat

Salmon Pasta Salad

Bread Sticks   *Sherbet & Cookies*

Seafood

◄ Veggie-Shrimp Stir-fry

1 pkg. (10 oz.) frozen broccoli cuts
1 cup julienne carrots (2 × ¼-inch strips)
2 tablespoons margarine or butter
½ teaspoon garlic powder
1 pkg. (10 oz.) frozen cooked shrimp, defrosted
   and drained
1 cup fresh snow pea pods
2 teaspoons cornstarch
¼ teaspoon ground ginger
2 tablespoons soy sauce
2 tablespoons water

4 servings

In 2-quart casserole, combine broccoli, carrots, margarine and garlic powder. Cover. Microwave at High for 6 to 8 minutes, or until broccoli is defrosted, stirring once to break apart. Add shrimp and pea pods. Mix well. Re-cover. Microwave at High for 6 to 8 minutes, or until hot, stirring once. Drain. Set aside.

In 1-cup measure, combine cornstarch and ginger. Blend in soy sauce and water. Microwave at High for 1 to 1½ minutes, or until sauce is thickened and translucent, stirring every 30 seconds. Add sauce to shrimp mixture. Toss to coat. Serve over hot cooked rice, if desired.

Per Serving: Calories: 286 • Protein: 21 g. • Carbohydrate: 36 g. • Fat: 7 g. • Cholesterol: 138 mg. • Sodium: 770 mg.
Exchanges: 1½ starch, 2 lean meat, 3 vegetable

Veggie-Shrimp Stir-fry

Sesame Seed Bread Sticks
Fresh Pineapple Slices

Scallop Salad Sensational

1 lb. bay scallops, rinsed and drained
1 tablespoon plus 1 teaspoon lime juice,
   divided
1 cup seeded chopped tomato
⅓ cup seeded chopped cucumber
⅓ cup mayonnaise
⅓ cup sour cream
2 tablespoons grated Parmesan cheese
¼ teaspoon garlic powder

4 servings

Arrange scallops in 8-inch square baking dish. Cover with plastic wrap.

Microwave at High for 4½ to 6 minutes, or until scallops are firm and opaque, stirring twice. Drain. Sprinkle scallops with 2 teaspoons lime juice. Add tomato and cucumber. Toss to combine.

In small mixing bowl, combine mayonnaise, sour cream, Parmesan cheese, garlic powder and the remaining 2 teaspoons lime juice. Arrange scallop mixture on 4 lettuce-lined plates. Top evenly with dressing.

Per Serving: Calories: 303 • Protein: 22 g. • Carbohydrate: 7 g. • Fat: 21 g. • Cholesterol: 60 mg. • Sodium: 362 mg.
Exchanges: 3 lean meat, 1½ vegetable, 2½ fat

Scallop Salad Sensational

Baguettes
Brownies

Quick Clam Chowder ▲

⅓ cup sliced green onions
2 tablespoons margarine or butter
2 cans (10¾ oz. each) condensed cream
   of potato soup
2⅔ cups milk
1 can (6½ oz.) minced clams, drained
1 teaspoon dried parsley flakes

4 to 6 servings

In 2-quart casserole, place onions and margarine. Cover. Microwave at High for 1½ to 2 minutes, or until onions are tender. Add remaining ingredients. Mix well. Re-cover. Microwave at High for 7 to 9 minutes, or until hot, stirring twice. Garnish with shredded carrot, if desired.

Per Serving: Calories: 195 • Protein: 13 g. • Carbohydrate: 16 g. • Fat: 8 g. • Cholesterol: 34 mg. • Sodium: 943 mg.
Exchanges: ½ starch, 1 lean meat, ½ vegetable, ½ low-fat milk, ½ fat

Quick Clam Chowder

Crackers   Green & Red Grapes

Cheesy Shrimp & Broccoli

2 pkgs. (10 oz. each) frozen broccoli in cheese-
   flavored sauce
2 cans (4½ oz. each) small deveined shrimp,
   rinsed and drained
¼ teaspoon dried dill weed
⅓ cup crushed buttery cracker crumbs (about
   8 crackers)

4 servings

Remove frozen broccoli from pouches. Place in 2-quart casserole. Cover. Microwave at High for 8 to 12 minutes, or until hot.

Add shrimp and dill weed. Mix well. Sprinkle with cracker crumbs. Microwave at High for 4 to 6 minutes, or until hot, rotating casserole once.

Per Serving: Calories: 189 • Protein: 19 g. • Carbohydrate: 16 g. • Fat: 5 g. • Cholesterol: 111 mg. • Sodium: 835 mg.
Exchanges: ½ starch, 2 lean meat, 2 vegetable, ½ fat

Cheesy Shrimp & Broccoli

Dinner Rolls   Chocolate Cake

Crab-Asparagus Melts

2 cans (6 oz. each) crab meat,
    rinsed, drained and
    cartilage removed
⅓ cup mayonnaise
¼ cup sliced green onions
2 tablespoons unseasoned dry
    bread crumbs
1 teaspoon lemon juice
½ pkg. (10 oz.) frozen
    asparagus cuts
3 English muffins, split and
    toasted
½ cup pasteurized process
    cheese spread

6 servings

In medium mixing bowl, combine
crab meat, mayonnaise, onions,
bread crumbs and lemon juice.
Set aside.

In small mixing bowl, microwave
asparagus cuts at High for 2 to
3 minutes, or until defrosted, stirring once to break apart. Drain.
Add asparagus to crab mixture.
Mix well.

Arrange English muffin halves
on paper-towel-lined plate. Top
evenly with crab mixture. Microwave at High for 2 to 3 minutes,
or until hot, rotating plate once.

Place cheese spread in 1-cup
measure. Microwave at High
for 30 seconds to 1 minute, or
until cheese is melted and can
be stirred smooth, stirring once.
Spoon cheese sauce evenly over
crab mixture.

Per Serving: Calories: 280 • Protein: 17 g.
• Carbohydrate: 20 g. • Fat: 15 g. •
Cholesterol: 55 mg. • Sodium: 540 mg.
Exchanges: 1 starch, 2 medium-fat meat,
1 fat

Crab-Asparagus Melts

Iced Coffee

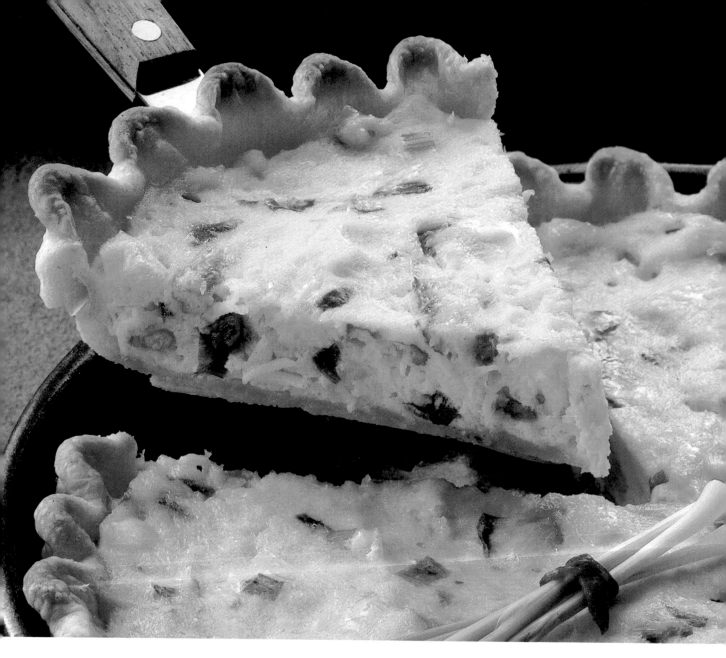

Crab Quiche

½ pkg. (15 oz.) refrigerated
    prepared pie crust
¼ cup sliced green onions
2 tablespoons margarine or
    butter
1 tablespoon all-purpose flour
¼ teaspoon salt
4 eggs
1 can (6 oz.) crab meat, rinsed,
    drained and cartilage
    removed
½ cup shredded Cheddar
    cheese
½ cup milk
1 tablespoon diced pimiento,
    drained

4 to 6 servings

Prepare pie crust as directed on package for single crust. Set aside.

In 1½-quart casserole, combine onions and margarine. Cover. Microwave at High for 1 to 1½ minutes, or until onions are tender. Stir in flour and salt. Add remaining ingredients. Mix well. Microwave filling at High for 3 to 5 minutes, or until mixture is hot and begins to set around edges, stirring twice with whisk.

Pour into prepared crust. Microwave at High for 8 to 10 minutes, or until center of filling is set, rotating twice. Let stand for 5 minutes.

Per Serving: Calories: 486 • Protein: 15 g. • Carbohydrate: 32 g. • Fat: 33 g.
• Cholesterol: 171 mg. • Sodium: 715 mg.
Exchanges: 2 starch, 1 medium-fat meat, ½ vegetable, 5½ fat

Crab Quiche

Fresh Fruit Salad   *Muffins*

Shrimp & Egg Croissants ▲

    4 eggs
   ⅓ cup milk
   ¼ teaspoon salt
   ¼ cup sliced green onions
    1 can (6 oz.) small deveined shrimp, rinsed and
       drained
    4 croissants, split
   ⅓ cup shredded Cheddar cheese

4 servings

In 1-quart casserole, combine eggs, milk and salt. Blend with whisk. Add onions. Mix well. Cover. Microwave at High for 4 to 5½ minutes, or until eggs are set, stirring twice to break apart. Add shrimp. Mix well.

Place bottom halves of croissants on paper-towel-lined plate. Spoon ½ cup egg mixture evenly over each croissant half. Sprinkle evenly with cheese. Top with remaining croissant halves. Cover with paper towel. Microwave at High for 1 to 1½ minutes, or until croissants are hot and cheese is melted.

Per Serving: Calories: 346 • Protein: 22 g. • Carbohydrate: 22 g. • Fat: 18 g. • Cholesterol: 294 mg. • Sodium: 467 mg.
Exchanges: 1½ starch, 2½ lean meat, 2 fat

Shrimp & Egg Croissants

Orange Juice

Savory Clams & Linguine

    8 oz. uncooked linguine
    1 pkg. (1.8 oz.) white sauce mix
   ⅛ teaspoon pepper
    2 cups milk
   ¼ cup green onions
    2 cans (6½ oz. each) minced clams, drained
       (reserve 1 tablespoon juice)
    1 tablespoon diced pimiento, drained

4 servings

Prepare linguine as directed on package. Rinse and drain. Set aside.

In 2-quart casserole, combine white sauce mix and pepper. Blend in milk with whisk. Add onions. Mix well. Microwave at High for 10 to 14 minutes, or until sauce thickens and bubbles, stirring twice.

Add clams, reserved 1 tablespoon juice and the pimiento. Mix well. Microwave at High for 2 to 3 minutes, or until hot. Serve over linguine.

Per Serving: Calories: 469 • Protein: 36 g. • Carbohydrate: 60 g. • Fat: 8 g. • Cholesterol: 71 mg. • Sodium: 601 mg.
Exchanges: 3½ starch, 3 lean meat, ½ vegetable, ½ low-fat milk

Savory Clams & Linguine

Garlic Toast   *Tossed Salad*

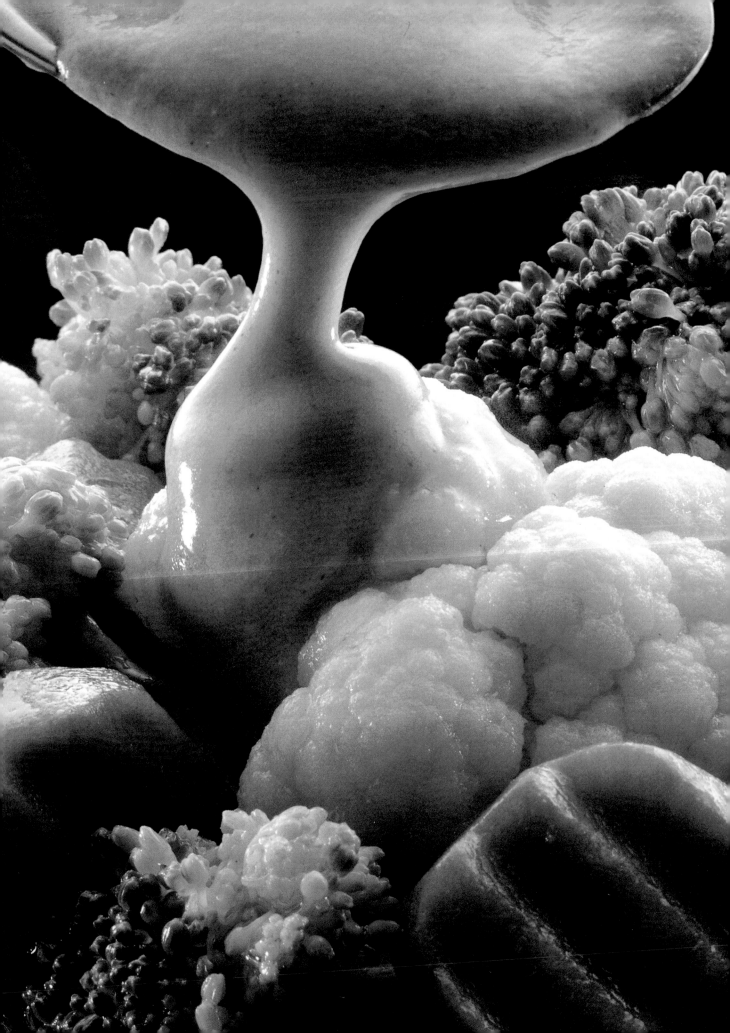

Super-quick Side Dishes

Country Vegetable Medley

◄ Oriental Sesame Broccoli

- 1 tablespoon margarine or butter
- 2 tablespoons sesame seed
- 1 medium onion, cut into ½-inch wedges
- 3 tablespoons teriyaki sauce
- 1 tablespoon sesame oil
- ½ teaspoon sugar
- ¼ teaspoon crushed red pepper flakes
- 1 pkg. (16 oz.) frozen broccoli cuts

4 servings

In 1-cup measure, microwave margarine at High for 30 to 45 seconds, or until melted. Stir in sesame seed. Microwave at High for 2 to 3 minutes, or until light golden brown, stirring after every minute. Let stand for 2 to 3 minutes (seeds will continue to toast during standing time). Drain seeds on paper-towel-lined plate. Set aside.

Place onion in 2-quart casserole. Cover. Microwave at High for 1½ to 2 minutes, or until tender. In small bowl, combine teriyaki sauce, sesame oil, sugar and red pepper flakes. Add teriyaki mixture and broccoli to onion. Toss to coat. Re-cover. Microwave at High for 7 to 8 minutes, or until broccoli is hot, stirring once. Sprinkle with sesame seed.

Per Serving: Calories: 129 • Protein: 5 g. • Carbohydrate: 11 g. • Fat: 9 g. • Cholesterol: 0 • Sodium: 579 mg.
Exchanges: 2 vegetable, 1½ fat

Country Vegetable Medley

- 1 tablespoon margarine or butter
- 2 teaspoons lemon juice
- 2 teaspoons stone-ground mustard
- ¼ teaspoon salt
- 1 pkg. (16 oz.) frozen broccoli, cauliflower and carrots
- ⅓ cup water

6 servings

In small bowl, microwave margarine at High for 45 seconds to 1 minute, or until melted. Add lemon juice, mustard and salt. Mix well. Set aside.

In 2-quart casserole, combine vegetables and water. Cover. Microwave at High for 8 to 11 minutes, or until hot, stirring once. Drain. Add margarine mixture. Toss to coat.

Per Serving: Calories: 41 • Protein: 2 g. • Carbohydrate: 5 g. • Fat: 2 g. • Cholesterol: 0 • Sodium: 156 mg.
Exchanges: 1 vegetable, ½ fat

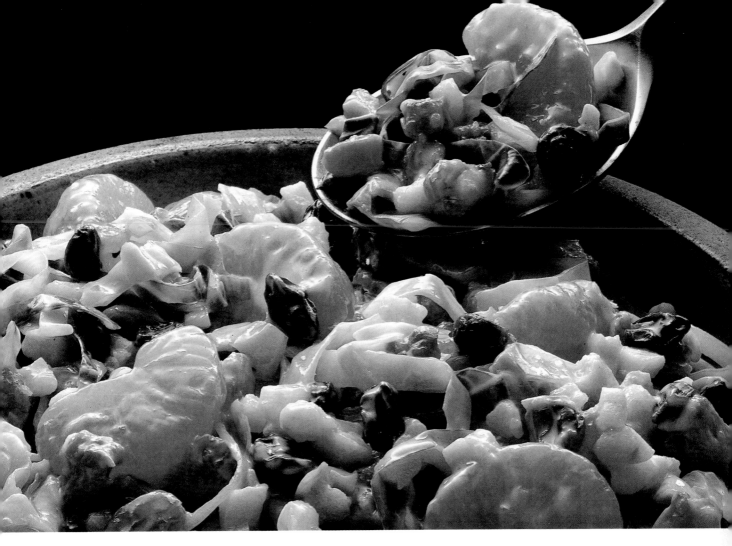

Warm Fruited Slaw ▲

3 cups shredded cabbage
1 pkg. (6 oz.) dried fruit bits
1 can (11 oz.) mandarin orange
　segments, drained (reserve
　¼ cup liquid)
⅛ teaspoon salt
½ cup orange-flavored low-fat
　yogurt
¼ teaspoon ground cinnamon

6 servings

In 2-quart casserole, combine
cabbage, fruit bits, reserved
mandarin orange liquid and the
salt. Cover. Microwave at High
for 3 to 4 minutes, or until cabbage is tender-crisp, stirring once.
Add oranges, yogurt and cinnamon. Toss gently to combine.
Serve immediately.

Per Serving: Calories: 117 • Protein: 2 g.
• Carbohydrate: 29 g. • Fat: 0 •
Cholesterol: 1 mg. • Sodium: 71 mg.
Exchanges: 2 vegetable 1 fruit

Blue Cheese
Cauliflower & Peas

1 pkg. (16 oz.) frozen
　cauliflowerets
1 cup frozen peas
⅓ cup water
1 jar (5 oz.) blue cheese-
　flavored cream cheese
　spread

6 servings

In 2-quart casserole, combine
cauliflower, peas and water. Cover.
Microwave at High for 10 to 13 minutes, or until hot, stirring once or
twice. Drain.

Add cream cheese spread. Re-
cover. Microwave at High for 2 to
4 minutes, or until melted, stirring
once to coat vegetables.

Per Serving: Calories: 105 • Protein: 7 g.
• Carbohydrate: 9 g. • Fat: 5 g.
• Cholesterol: 13 mg. • Sodium: 364 mg.
Exchanges: 1½ high-fat meat, 2 vegetable

Greek Beans & Tomatoes

1 pkg. (16 oz.) frozen whole
　green beans
2 tablespoons olive oil
1 clove garlic, minced
½ teaspoon dried basil leaves
¼ teaspoon salt
1 medium tomato, cut into
　8 wedges
2 tablespoons crumbled feta
　cheese

6 servings

In 2-quart casserole, combine all
ingredients, except tomato and
cheese. Cover. Microwave at
High for 8 to 10 minutes, or until
beans are hot, stirring once. Add
tomato. Toss gently to combine.
Sprinkle with cheese.

Per Serving: Calories: 75 • Protein: 2 g.
• Carbohydrate: 7 g. • Fat: 5 g.
• Cholesterol: 2 mg. • Sodium: 119 mg.
Exchanges: ½ starch, 1 fat

Corn & Spinach Medley

    1 pkg. (3 oz.) cream cheese
    1 tablespoon milk
   ¼ teaspoon salt
   ⅛ teaspoon garlic powder
    1 can (11 oz.) corn with red and
       green peppers, drained
    1 can (4 oz.) chopped green
       chilies, drained
    2 cups torn fresh spinach
       leaves

4 servings

In 2-quart casserole, combine
cream cheese, milk, salt and garlic powder. Microwave at High for
30 to 45 seconds, or until cheese
is softened. Stir mixture until
smooth. Stir in corn and chilies.
Microwave at High for 2 to 3 minutes, or until hot, stirring once. Stir
in spinach. Microwave at High for
1 to 1½ minutes, or until mixture
is hot and spinach is wilted.

Per Serving: Calories: 146 • Protein: 5 g.
• Carbohydrate: 16 g. • Fat: 8 g. •
Cholesterol: 24 mg. • Sodium: 441 mg.
Exchanges: 1 starch, 1½ fat

Hot Pepper Summer Squash ▲

    1 tablespoon margarine or butter
  1½ cups sliced yellow summer squash
  1½ cups sliced zucchini squash
   ½ teaspoon dried oregano leaves
   ¼ teaspoon salt
   ½ cup shredded hot pepper Monterey
       Jack cheese

4 servings

In 2-quart casserole, microwave margarine at High
for 45 seconds to 1 minute, or until melted. Stir in
squashes, oregano and salt. Cover. Microwave at
High for 4 to 6 minutes, or until squashes are
tender-crisp, stirring once.

Stir in cheese. Re-cover. Let stand for 1 minute, or
until cheese is melted. Before serving, toss gently.

Per Serving: Calories: 95 • Protein: 5 g. • Carbohydrate: 7 g.
• Fat: 13 g. • Cholesterol: 13 mg. • Sodium: 245 mg.
Exchanges: 1 vegetable, 1½ fat

Cream-style Peppers & Corn

    1 tablespoon margarine or butter
   ½ teaspoon fennel seed, crushed
   ⅛ teaspoon garlic powder
   ⅛ teaspoon salt
    1 medium green pepper, cut into ¼-inch strips
    1 medium red pepper, cut into ¼-inch strips
    1 cup frozen corn
   ¼ cup sour cream

4 servings

In 2-quart casserole, combine margarine, fennel
seed, garlic powder and salt. Microwave at High
for 45 seconds to 1 minute, or until margarine is
melted. Add peppers and corn. Toss to coat. Cover.
Microwave at High for 4 to 6 minutes, or until peppers are tender-crisp, stirring once. Add sour cream.
Toss to coat.

Per Serving: Calories: 110 • Protein: 2 g. • Carbohydrate: 13 g.
• Fat: 7 g. • Cholesterol: 7 mg. • Sodium: 112 mg.
Exchanges: ½ starch, 1 vegetable, 1 fat

Julienne Carrots & Beets ▶

2 tablespoons horseradish
2 teaspoons packed brown
   sugar
1 teaspoon grated orange peel
1 can (16 oz.) julienne beets,
   rinsed and drained
1 can (16 oz.) julienne carrots,
   rinsed and drained

6 servings

In small bowl, combine horseradish, sugar and peel. Mix well.
Set aside. In 2-quart casserole,
combine beets and carrots. Cover.
Microwave at High for 3 to 6 minutes, or until hot, stirring once. Add
horseradish mixture. Toss to coat.

Per Serving: Calories: 34 • Protein: 1 g.
• Carbohydrate: 8 g. • Fat: 0 •
Cholesterol: 0 • Sodium: 254 mg.
Exchanges: 1½ vegetable

Spicy Glazed Carrots ▶

1 pkg. (16 oz.) frozen crinkle-
   cut carrots
¼ cup apricot preserves
1 tablespoon water
¼ teaspoon chili powder
¼ teaspoon salt
⅛ teaspoon ground ginger
   Dash cayenne

6 servings

In 2-quart casserole, combine all
ingredients. Cover. Microwave at
High for 7 to 10 minutes, or until
carrots are hot, stirring once.

Per Serving: Calories: 64 • Protein: 1 g.
• Carbohydrate: 16 g. • Fat: 0 •
Cholesterol: 0 • Sodium: 136 mg.
Exchanges: 1½ vegetable, ½ fruit

Cajun Pasta

4 oz. uncooked linguine
2 teaspoons olive oil
1 can (8 oz.) whole tomatoes, undrained and cut up
1 cup thinly sliced celery

½ teaspoon dried oregano leaves
½ teaspoon sugar
¼ teaspoon salt
¼ teaspoon garlic powder

4 servings

Prepare linguine as directed on package. Rinse and drain. Add oil. Toss to coat. Set aside.

In 2-quart casserole, combine remaining ingredients. Mix well. Cover. Microwave at High for 3 to 6 minutes, or until celery is tender-crisp, stirring once.

Add linguine to tomato mixture. Toss to coat. Re-cover. Microwave at High for 2 minutes, or until hot.

Per Serving: Calories: 145 • Protein: 4 g. • Carbohydrate: 26 g. • Fat: 3 g.
• Cholesterol: 0 • Sodium: 253 mg.
Exchanges: 1 starch, 2 vegetable, ½ fat

Pasta Side Dishes

◀ Pasta with Spinach

8 oz. uncooked rotini
¼ cup sliced green onions
2 tablespoons olive oil
1 pkg. (10 oz.) frozen chopped spinach
1 jar (5 oz.) sharp pasteurized process cheese spread
1 jar (2 oz.) diced pimiento, drained

4 to 6 servings

Prepare rotini as directed on package. Rinse and drain. Set aside.

In 2-quart casserole, combine onions and oil. Cover. Microwave at High for 1 to 1½ minutes, or until onions are tender. Add rotini to onion mixture. Toss to coat. Re-cover. Set aside.

Place spinach in 1½-quart casserole. Cover. Microwave at High for 6 to 7 minutes, or until hot, stirring once to break apart. Drain, pressing to remove excess moisture. Stir in cheese spread. Microwave at High for 1 to 2 minutes, or until cheese is melted, stirring once. Spoon spinach mixture over rotini mixture. Sprinkle with pimiento.

Per Serving: Calories: 263 • Protein: 10 g.
• Carbohydrate: 33 g. • Fat: 10 g.
• Cholesterol: 13 mg. • Sodium: 355 mg.
Exchanges: 1½ starch, 2 vegetable, 2 fat

Italian Orzo with Olives ▶

8 oz. uncooked rosamarina
  (orzo) pasta
¼ cup white vinegar
2 teaspoons grated orange
  peel
2 tablespoons orange juice
1 pkg. (0.6 oz.) zesty Italian
  dressing mix
½ cup vegetable oil
½ cup sliced black olives
  Leaf lettuce
1 medium orange, peeled and
  chopped

8 servings

Prepare rosamarina as directed
on package. Rinse and drain.
Set aside.

In medium mixing bowl, combine
vinegar, orange peel, orange juice
and dressing mix. Blend in oil
with whisk.

Add rosamarina. Toss to coat.
Microwave at High for 2 to 4 minutes, or until hot, stirring once.
Stir in olives. Serve on leaf lettuce. Garnish each serving with
chopped oranges.

Per Serving: Calories: 253 • Protein: 4 g.
• Carbohydrate: 26 g. • Fat: 15 g. •
Cholesterol: 0 • Sodium: 356 mg.
Exchanges: 1 starch, ½ fruit, 3 fat

Vegetable Couscous

1⅓ cups water
1 pkg. (9 oz.) frozen mixed
  vegetables
1 tablespoon instant minced
  onion
½ teaspoon instant chicken
  bouillon granules
¼ teaspoon dried thyme
  leaves
⅛ teaspoon garlic powder
1 cup uncooked couscous
1 tablespoon lemon juice

4 servings

In 2-quart casserole, combine all ingredients, except couscous and
lemon juice. Cover. Microwave at High for 9 to 12 minutes, or until
water begins to boil.

Stir in couscous and lemon juice. Re-cover. Let stand for 5 minutes.
Fluff with fork.

Per Serving: Calories: 196 • Protein: 7 g. • Carbohydrate: 40 g. • Fat: 0
• Cholesterol: 0 • Sodium: 159 mg.
Exchanges: 2 starch, 2 vegetable

Rice with Beans & Jalapeños

1	cup hot water
½	cup picante sauce
½	cup sliced green onions
1	tablespoon margarine or butter
1½	cups uncooked instant rice
1	can (16 oz.) pinto beans, rinsed and drained
1	tablespoon canned diced jalapeño peppers
1	medium tomato, cut into 8 wedges

6 servings

In 2-quart casserole, combine water, picante sauce, onions and margarine. Cover. Microwave at High for 4 to 6 minutes, or until water begins to boil.

Stir in rice, beans and peppers. Re-cover. Let stand for 5 minutes. Before serving, fluff rice with fork. Garnish with tomato wedges.

Per Serving: Calories: 181 • Protein: 6 g. • Carbohydrate: 34 g. • Fat: 2 g. • Cholesterol: 0 • Sodium: 178 mg. Exchanges: 1 vegetable, ½ fat

Polynesian Pilaf ▲

- 1 can (8 oz.) pineapple tidbits in juice
- 2 cups uncooked instant rice
- 1 pkg. (6 oz.) frozen pea pods
- 2 tablespoons soy sauce
- 1 tablespoon packed brown sugar
- 2 teaspoons diced pimiento, drained
- ¼ teaspoon salt

4 servings

Drain pineapple juice into 2-cup measure. Add hot water to equal 1⅔ cups. In 2-quart casserole, combine juice mixture and remaining ingredients. Cover. Microwave at High for 10 to 12 minutes, or just until rice is tender and liquid is absorbed. Let stand, covered, for 2 to 4 minutes. Before serving, fluff rice with fork.

Per Serving: Calories: 246 • Protein: 5 g. • Carbohydrate: 56 g. • Fat: 0 • Cholesterol: 0 • Sodium: 654 mg.
Exchanges: 2 starch, 1½ fruit

Lemon-Rosemary Rice

- 2 cups uncooked instant rice
- 1⅔ cups hot water
- 1 teaspoon margarine or butter
- 1 teaspoon grated lemon peel
- ½ teaspoon dried rosemary leaves, crushed
- ½ teaspoon salt

6 servings

In 2-quart casserole, combine all ingredients. Cover. Microwave at High for 6 to 8 minutes, or until rice is tender and liquid is absorbed. Let stand, covered, for 2 to 4 minutes. Before serving, fluff rice with fork.

Per Serving: Calories: 124 • Protein: 2 g. • Carbohydrate: 26 g. • Fat: 1 g. • Cholesterol: 0 • Sodium: 185 mg.
Exchanges: 1½ starch

Quick Curried Rice

- 2 cups uncooked instant rice
- 1⅔ cups hot water
- ½ cup raisins
- ¼ cup slivered almonds
- 2 teaspoons dried parsley flakes
- 1 teaspoon curry powder
- 1 teaspoon margarine or butter

6 servings

In 2-quart casserole, combine all ingredients. Cover. Microwave at High for 6 to 8 minutes, or until rice is tender and liquid is absorbed. Let stand, covered, for 2 to 4 minutes. Before serving, fluff rice with fork.

Per Serving: Calories: 218 • Protein: 5 g. • Carbohydrate: 38 g. • Fat: 6 g. • Cholesterol: 0 • Sodium: 11 mg.
Exchanges: 2 starch, ½ fruit, 1 fat

◀ Herb-crusted Potatoes

¼ cup margarine or butter,
  divided
½ cup herb-seasoned stuffing
  mix, finely crushed
2 tablespoons grated
  Parmesan cheese
2 teaspoons dried parsley
  flakes
4 russet potatoes (about 4 oz.
  each), peeled

4 servings

In small mixing bowl, microwave 2 tablespoons margarine at High for 45 seconds to 1 minute, or until melted. Add stuffing mix, cheese and parsley. Mix well. Set aside.

In small bowl, microwave remaining 2 tablespoons margarine at High for 45 seconds to 1 minute, or until melted.

Roll each potato in margarine, then in stuffing mixture. Arrange on 9-inch pie plate. Drizzle any remaining margarine over coated potatoes.

Cover with paper towel. Microwave at High for 6 to 8 minutes, or until potatoes are tender, rotating pie plate once.

Per Serving: Calories: 271 • Protein: 6 g.
• Carbohydrate: 33 g. • Fat: 13 g.
• Cholesterol: 3 mg. • Sodium: 433 mg.
Exchanges: 2 starch, ½ vegetable, 2½ fat

Garlic-Thyme Potato Puff

1¾ cups hot water
 ½ teaspoon garlic powder
 ½ teaspoon dried thyme leaves
 ¼ teaspoon salt
  2 cups instant mashed potato
    flakes

1 cup half-and-half
1 cup shredded Cheddar
  cheese, divided
1 egg, beaten

6 servings

In 1½-quart soufflé dish or casserole, combine water, garlic powder, thyme and salt. Cover with plastic wrap. Microwave at High for 5 to 8 minutes, or until water begins to boil.

Add potato flakes, half-and-half and ½ cup of cheese. Stir until mixture thickens. Add egg. Mix well. Microwave at High, uncovered, for 8 to 10 minutes, or until mixture is set.

Sprinkle with remaining ½ cup cheese. Microwave at High for 1 to 1½ minutes, or until cheese is melted.

Per Serving: Calories: 198 • Protein: 8 g. • Carbohydrate: 15 g. • Fat: 12 g.
• Cholesterol: 80 mg. • Sodium: 255 mg.
Exchanges: 1 starch, ½ high-fat meat, 1½ fat

Warm New Potato Salad ▲

⅓ cup plain low-fat yogurt
1 tablespoon snipped fresh
   cilantro leaves
1 tablespoon Dijon mustard
½ teaspoon sugar
⅛ teaspoon salt

1 lb. new potatoes, cut into
   quarters (about 3 cups)
2 tablespoons water
2 cups frozen broccoli, green
   beans, pearl onions and red
   pepper vegetable mixture

6 servings

In 1-cup measure, combine yogurt, cilantro, mustard, sugar and salt.
Mix well. Set aside.

In 2-quart casserole, combine potatoes and water. Cover. Microwave at High for 6 to 11 minutes, or until potatoes are almost tender,
stirring once.

Stir in vegetable mixture. Re-cover. Microwave at High for 4 to 7 minutes, or until potatoes are tender and vegetables are hot. Drain. Add
yogurt mixture. Toss gently to coat.

Per Serving: Calories: 97 • Protein: 4 g. • Carbohydrate: 20 g. • Fat: 1 g.
• Cholesterol: 1 mg. • Sodium: 139 mg.
Exchanges: 1 starch, 1 vegetable

Cucumber Potato Salad

2 cups frozen hash brown
   potato cubes with chopped
   onions and peppers
¼ cup water
1 medium cucumber, seeded
   and cut into 1½ × ½-inch
   strips
¼ cup creamy cucumber
   dressing

4 servings

In 4-cup measure, combine potatoes and water. Microwave at High
for 3 to 6 minutes, or until hot, stirring once. Drain.

Add cucumber and dressing. Stir
gently. Serve warm or cold.

Per Serving: Calories: 149 • Protein: 2 g.
• Carbohydrate: 21 g. • Fat: 7 g. •
Cholesterol: 0 • Sodium: 211 mg.
Exchanges: 1 starch, 1½ vegetable, 1 fat

Speedy Gourmet

Fast & Fancy Salad Supper

Warm Fruit & Nut Brie   Caesar-style Tortellini Salad
Lemon Sherbet & Cookies*

Warm Fruit & Nut Brie

1 wheel (8 oz.) chilled Brie
    cheese, 4½ × 1½ inches
⅓ cup apricot preserves,
    divided
1 pkg. (2 oz.) cashews,
    coarsely chopped, divided

Crackers
Fresh fruit (grapes, apple and
    pear slices)

6 servings

Cut Brie in half crosswise. Place bottom half cut-side-up in center of serving plate. Spoon half of preserves evenly over bottom half of Brie. Sprinkle with half of cashews. Cover with top half of Brie. Press together. Microwave at 50% (Medium) for 1 to 1½ minutes, or until cheese is warm and spreadable, rotating once. Spread top of Brie with remaining preserves. Sprinkle with remaining cashews. Serve with crackers and fresh fruit. Garnish with whole cashews, if desired.

Per Serving: Calories: 226 • Protein: 9 g. • Carbohydrate: 15 g. • Fat: 15 g.
• Cholesterol: 38 mg. • Sodium: 301 mg.
Exchanges: 1½ high-fat meat, 1 fruit, ½ fat

Caesar-style Tortellini Salad

1 pkg. (9 oz.) uncooked fresh
    cheese-filled tortellini
1 cup fresh broccoli flowerettes
1 cup julienne carrots (2 × ¼-
    inch strips)
1 cup cherry tomatoes
1 jar (6 oz.) marinated
    artichoke hearts, drained

½ cup Italian dressing
2 tablespoons margarine or
    butter
3 cups cubed rye bread (1-inch
    cubes)
⅛ teaspoon garlic powder
3 cups torn romaine lettuce

6 servings

Prepare tortellini as directed on package. Rinse and drain. Set aside. In 1-quart casserole, place broccoli and carrots. Cover. Microwave at High for 2 to 3 minutes, or until tender-crisp, stirring once. Drain. In large mixing bowl or salad bowl, combine tortellini, vegetables and dressing. Toss to coat. Cover with plastic wrap. Chill 1 to 2 hours.

In 11 × 7-inch baking dish, microwave margarine at High for 45 seconds to 1 minute, or until melted. Add bread cubes. Toss to coat. Sprinkle with garlic powder. Microwave at High for 6 to 7 minutes, or until bread cubes are crisp, stirring twice. Cool. Add bread cubes and lettuce to chilled salad. Mix well. Serve immediately.

Per Serving: Calories: 325 • Protein: 10 g. • Carbohydrate: 33 g. • Fat: 18 g.
• Cholesterol: 51 mg. • Sodium: 529 mg.
Exchanges: 1½ starch, ½ high-fat meat, 2 vegetable, 2½ fat

Sausage Brunch Pie

- 8 oz. fresh pork sausage
- 8 eggs
- ⅓ cup milk
- 1 tablespoon all-purpose flour
- ½ teaspoon freeze-dried chives
- ½ teaspoon onion salt
- ½ teaspoon dried parsley flakes
- ½ cup shredded Cheddar cheese, divided
- 1 large tomato, cut into 8 wedges

6 servings

Lightly grease 10-inch deep-dish pie plate. Set aside. Crumble sausage into 1-quart casserole. Cover with wax paper or microwave cooking paper. Microwave at High for 3 to 4 minutes, or until meat is no longer pink, stirring twice to break apart. Drain. Set aside.

In 8-cup measure, combine eggs, milk, flour, chives, onion salt and parsley flakes. Beat with whisk until blended. Microwave egg mixture at 70% (Medium High) for 6 to 8 minutes, or just until eggs begin to set, stirring twice. Reserve 2 tablespoons cheese. Add remaining cheese and the sausage to egg mixture. Mix well. Pour into prepared pie plate.

Place pie plate on saucer in oven. Microwave at 70% (Medium High) for 9 to 11 minutes, or until mixture is set in center, rotating every 3 minutes. Arrange tomato wedges on top of pie. Sprinkle reserved cheese over tomatoes. Microwave at High for 1 to 2 minutes, or until cheese is melted. Let stand for 5 minutes.

Per Serving: Calories: 223 • Protein: 15 g. • Carbohydrate: 4 g. • Fat: 16 g. • Cholesterol: 311 mg. • Sodium: 520 mg.
Exchanges: 2 high-fat meat, 1 vegetable

Tangy Warm Fruit Cup

- 3 cans (11 oz. each) pineapple and mandarin orange segments, drained
- 2 cups seedless red grapes
- 3 tablespoons frozen orange juice concentrate, defrosted
- ⅛ teaspoon ground nutmeg

6 servings

In 2-quart casserole, combine all ingredients. Cover. Microwave at High for 5 to 6 minutes, or until mixture is hot, stirring once. Spoon evenly into individual serving dishes. Sprinkle with flaked coconut, if desired.

Per Serving: Calories: 84 • Protein: 1 g. • Carbohydrate: 21 g. • Fat: 0 • Cholesterol: 0 • Sodium: 2 mg.
Exchanges: 1½ fruit

Sweet Cinnamon Butter

- ½ cup margarine or butter
- 2 tablespoons powdered sugar
- ¼ teaspoon ground cinnamon

24 servings,
1 teaspoon each

In small mixing bowl, microwave margarine at 30% (Medium Low) for 15 seconds to 1 minute, or until softened. Add sugar and cinnamon. Beat at medium speed of electric mixer until fluffy. Store, covered, in refrigerator no longer than 2 weeks.

Per Serving: Calories: 36 • Protein: 0 • Carbohydrate: 1 g. • Fat: 4 g. • Cholesterol: 0 • Sodium: 45 mg.
Exchanges: 1 fat

Open-face Turkey Tomato Sandwiches

½ cup mayonnaise
1½ teaspoons prepared
    mustard
¼ teaspoon garlic powder
¼ teaspoon dried parsley
    flakes
4 slices sourdough bread
    (1 inch thick), toasted
½ lb. thinly sliced fully cooked
    turkey breast
1 medium tomato, sliced
    (8 slices)

4 servings

In small mixing bowl, combine mayonnaise, mustard, garlic powder and parsley flakes.

Place toasted bread slices on paper-towel-lined plate. Spread each with 1 tablespoon mayonnaise mixture. Top each with 1 or 2 turkey slices and 2 tomato slices. Cover with paper towel. Microwave at 70% (Medium High) for 3½ to 5 minutes, or until sandwiches are warm, rotating plate once. Spoon remaining mayonnaise mixture evenly over sandwiches. Garnish with parsley, if desired.

Per Serving: Calories: 382 • Protein: 21 g. • Carbohydrate: 21 g. • Fat: 23 g.
• Cholesterol: 64 mg. • Sodium: 414 mg.
Exchanges: 1 starch, 2 lean meat, 1 vegetable, 3½ fat

Fruit Medley with Lime Dressing

2 oranges, peeled and sectioned
2 kiwifruit, peeled and sliced
2 medium bananas, cut in half lengthwise
    and sliced
½ cup seedless red grapes
¼ cup frozen limeade concentrate, defrosted
¼ cup vegetable oil
2 tablespoons water

4 servings

In medium mixing bowl, combine fruits. Toss gently. In 1-cup measure, combine remaining ingredients. Pour over fruit. Cover with plastic wrap. Chill 2 hours. Stir. Serve on lettuce-lined plates, if desired.

Per Serving: Calories: 276 • Protein: 2 g. • Carbohydrate: 40 g.
• Fat: 14 g. • Cholesterol: 0 • Sodium: 3 mg.
Exchanges: 2½ fruit, 3 fat

Chocolate Angel Parfaits

1 pkg. (3½ oz.) chocolate pudding and pie filling
2 cups milk
2 cups baked, cubed angel food cake
    Whipped cream

4 servings

Place pudding in 8-cup measure. Blend in milk with whisk. Microwave at High for 6 to 8 minutes, or until mixture thickens and bubbles, stirring twice with whisk. Place a piece of plastic wrap directly on surface of pudding. Chill 2 hours, or until cool. Layer pudding and cake pieces in parfait glasses. Top with whipped cream. Garnish with chocolate curls, if desired.

Per Serving: Calories: 217 • Protein: 6 g. • Carbohydrate: 42 g.
• Fat: 4 g. • Cholesterol: 13 mg. • Sodium: 205 mg.
Exchanges: 1½ starch, 1 fruit, ½ low-fat milk

Simple Pasta Dinner

Pasta Primavera   *Spiced Apple-Nut Salad*   *Spumoni**

Pasta Primavera

   1   pkg. (9 oz.) uncooked
         fettucini
   2   tablespoons margarine or
         butter
   2   tablespoons Worcestershire
         sauce
   ½   teaspoon garlic salt
   1   cup sliced fresh mushrooms
   1   cup quartered yellow
         summer squash slices
   1   cup sliced zucchini squash
   ½   medium tomato, cut into thin
         wedges
   3   tablespoons all-purpose
         flour
   1½   cups milk
   ¼   cup shredded fresh
         Parmesan cheese

                    6 servings

Prepare fettucini as directed on package. Rinse and drain. Place on serving platter. Cover with plastic wrap. Set aside.

In 1½-quart casserole, combine margarine, Worcestershire sauce and garlic salt. Microwave at High for 1 to 1½ minutes, or until margarine is melted. Add mushrooms and squashes. Cover. Microwave at High for 3 to 4 minutes, or until vegetables are tender, stirring once. Add tomato wedges. Re-cover. Microwave at High for 1 to 1½ minutes, or until hot.

Using slotted spoon, spoon vegetables over fettucini. Stir flour into reserved liquid in casserole. Blend in milk. Microwave at High for 6 to 8 minutes, or until mixture thickens and bubbles, stirring twice. Microwave vegetables and fettucini at High for 3 to 4 minutes, or until hot. Pour sauce over vegetables. Sprinkle with cheese.

Per Serving: Calories: 271 • Protein: 10 g. • Carbohydrate: 41 g. • Fat: 7 g.
• Cholesterol: 8 mg. • Sodium: 365 mg.
Exchanges: 1½ starch, 2½ vegetable, ½ low-fat milk, 1 fat

Spiced Apple-Nut Salad

   2   tablespoons sugar
   ½   cup pecan halves
   3   cups torn curly endive lettuce
   3   cups torn leaf lettuce
   2   small Rome apples, cored
         and thinly sliced
   ⅓   cup sliced green onions
   ¼   cup vegetable oil
   ¼   cup frozen apple juice
         concentrate, defrosted
   2   tablespoons white wine
         vinegar
   1   tablespoon sugar
   ¼   teaspoon ground cinnamon

                    6 servings

Lightly grease 12-inch square of foil. Set aside. Place sugar in small, heavy-gauge skillet. Cook conventionally over medium-high heat until sugar melts and becomes golden in color, stirring frequently. Remove from heat. Add pecans, tossing to coat. Immediately spoon nuts onto prepared foil. Cool completely. Break apart. Set aside.

In large mixing bowl or salad bowl, combine greens, apples and onions. In 1-cup measure, combine remaining ingredients. Pour over greens mixture. Toss to coat. Add pecans. Serve immediately.

Per Serving: Calories: 218 • Protein: 2 g. • Carbohydrate: 21 g. • Fat: 16 g.
• Cholesterol: 0 • Sodium: 15 mg.
Exchanges: 1 vegetable, 1 fruit, 3 fat

Oriental Express

Teriyaki Swordfish Steaks   *Jeweled Fried Rice*   *Caramel Fruit Dessert*

Teriyaki Swordfish Steaks

1 lb. fresh swordfish steaks,
    about 1 inch thick, cut into
    4 serving-size pieces
¼ cup teriyaki sauce
1 teaspoon sesame oil
½ teaspoon grated orange peel
¼ teaspoon garlic powder

4 servings

Arrange steaks in 11 × 7-inch baking dish. In 1-cup measure, combine remaining ingredients. Pour over steaks. Cover with plastic wrap. Marinate in refrigerator about 1 hour, turning steaks over once. Remove plastic wrap. Cover with wax paper or microwave cooking paper. Microwave at 70% (Medium High) for 8 to 13 minutes, or until fish flakes easily with fork, rearranging and turning over once.

Per Serving: Calories: 147 • Protein: 21 g. • Carbohydrate: 3 g. • Fat: 5 g.
• Cholesterol: 39 mg. • Sodium: 780 mg.
Exchanges: 3 lean meat, ½ vegetable

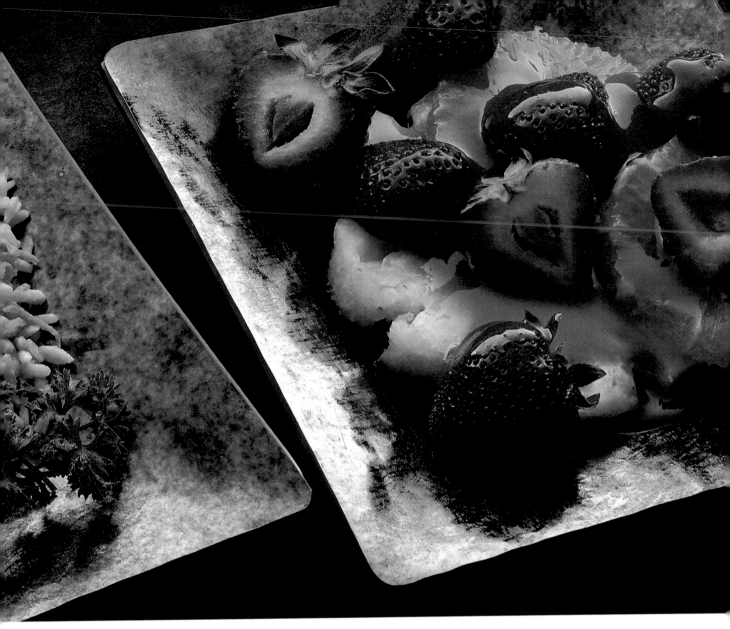

Jeweled Fried Rice

1½ cups uncooked instant rice
1½ cups hot water
½ cup shredded carrot
¼ cup sliced green onions
 2 tablespoons soy sauce
 2 teaspoons margarine or butter
½ teaspoon garlic powder
 2 tablespoons sliced almonds

4 servings

In 2-quart casserole, combine all ingredients, except almonds. Cover. Microwave at High for 4 to 8 minutes, or until rice is tender and liquid is absorbed. Let stand, covered, for 5 minutes. Fluff with fork. Sprinkle with almonds.

Per Serving: Calories: 181 • Protein: 4 g. • Carbohydrate: 33 g. • Fat: 4 g. • Cholesterol: 0 • Sodium: 543 mg.
Exchanges: 2 starch, ½ vegetable, ½ fat

Caramel Fruit Dessert

½ fresh pineapple, cored, peeled and sliced
 1 orange, peeled and sliced
 1 cup sliced fresh strawberries
⅓ cup caramel ice cream topping

4 servings

In medium mixing bowl, combine fruits. Toss gently. Set aside. In 1-cup measure, microwave caramel topping at High for 45 seconds to 1 minute, or until hot. Stir. Pour topping over fruit.

Per Serving: Calories: 129 • Protein: 2 g. • Carbohydrate: 31 g. • Fat: 1 g. • Cholesterol: 0 • Sodium: 52 mg.
Exchanges: 2 starch, ½ vegetable, ½ fat

Make-ahead Icebox Supper

Toasted Sesame & Seafood Salad　*Chilled Asparagus & Tomato Platter*
Lemon Garlic Crisps　*Assorted Sorbets**

Toasted Sesame & Seafood Salad

- 12 oz. uncooked spaghetti
- ½ lb. medium shrimp, shelled and deveined
- ½ lb. bay scallops
- ½ cup julienne carrot (2 × ⅛-inch strips)
- 1 cup julienne green and red pepper (2 × ⅛-inch strips)
- 1 tablespoon water
- ⅓ cup thinly sliced red onion
- 2 tablespoons sesame seed
- ¾ cup reduced-calorie mayonnaise
- ¼ cup milk
- 1 tablespoon soy sauce
- ¼ teaspoon crushed red pepper flakes

6 servings

Prepare spaghetti as directed on package. Rinse and drain. Set aside.

Arrange shrimp and scallops in even layer in 9-inch pie plate. Cover with plastic wrap. Microwave at 70% (Medium High) for 5 to 8 minutes, or until firm and opaque, stirring twice. Rinse with cold water. Drain. Set aside.

In 1-quart casserole, combine carrot, green and red peppers and water. Cover. Microwave at High for 2 to 3 minutes, or until vegetables are very hot and colors brighten. Rinse with cold water. Drain.

In large mixing bowl or salad bowl, combine spaghetti, shrimp and scallops, vegetable mixture and onion. Set aside.

Heat conventional oven to 350°F. Place sesame seed in even layer in 9-inch pie pan. Bake for 8 to 10 minutes, or until deep golden brown. In small mixing bowl, combine toasted sesame seed and remaining ingredients. Add to salad mixture. Toss to coat. Cover with plastic wrap. Chill about 2 hours, or until cold.

Per Serving: Calories: 396 • Protein: 21 g. • Carbohydrate: 50 g. • Fat: 12 g. • Cholesterol: 68 mg. • Sodium: 454 mg.
Exchanges: 2 starch, 1 lean meat, 4 vegetable, 2 fat

Chilled Asparagus & Tomato Platter

- 1 lb. fresh asparagus
- 2 tablespoons water
- 1 large tomato, cut into 6 slices
- ¼ cup chopped red onion
- ¼ cup olive oil
- 3 tablespoons red wine vinegar
- ¼ teaspoon instant minced garlic
- ¼ teaspoon freshly ground pepper
- ¼ teaspoon salt

6 servings

Arrange asparagus spears in 10-inch square casserole. Add water. Cover. Microwave at High for 6½ to 9½ minutes, or until asparagus is very hot and color brightens, rearranging spears once. Rinse spears with cold water. Drain. Arrange asparagus and tomato slices in casserole. Set aside. In 1-cup measure, combine remaining ingredients. Pour over asparagus and tomato. Cover. Chill at least 4 hours.

Per Serving: Calories: 104 • Protein: 3 g. • Carbohydrate: 5 g. • Fat: 9 g. • Cholesterol: 0 • Sodium: 93 mg.
Exchanges: 1 vegetable, 2 fat

Lemon Garlic Crisps

- 3 tablespoons margarine or butter
- ½ teaspoon lemon peel
- ¼ teaspoon garlic powder
- 12 thin slices baguette (¼-inch slices)

6 servings

In 8-inch square baking dish, microwave margarine at High for 1 to 1¼ minutes, or until melted. Add lemon peel and garlic powder. Mix well. Arrange baguette slices, slightly overlapping in dish, turning to coat with margarine mixture.

Microwave at High for 5 to 7 minutes, or until slices are crisp, turning slices over and rearranging after first 2 minutes and then after every minute.

Per Serving: Calories: 102 • Protein: 2 g. • Carbohydrate: 10 g. • Fat: 6 g. • Cholesterol: 1 mg. • Sodium: 169 mg.
Exchanges: ½ starch, 1 fat

Herbed Pork Medallions

¾- lb. pork tenderloin, sliced (½-inch slices)
1 cup orange juice
1 teaspoon dried rosemary leaves
½ teaspoon dried thyme leaves
¼ teaspoon salt
⅛ teaspoon pepper

4 servings

In 2-quart casserole, combine all ingredients. Cover. Marinate 1 hour in refrigerator. Microwave at High for 8 to 10 minutes, or until meat is no longer pink, stirring twice. Let pork stand, covered, for 5 minutes. Serve with slotted spoon.

Per Serving: Calories: 135 • Protein: 19 g. • Carbohydrate: 7 g. • Fat: 3 g. • Cholesterol: 59 mg. • Sodium: 177 mg.
Exchanges: 2½ lean meat, ½ fruit

Lemony New Potatoes

1½ lbs. small new potatoes
¼ cup water
¼ cup margarine or butter
1 tablespoon fresh lemon juice

4 servings

Remove thin strip of peel from center of each potato. Place potatoes and water in 1½-quart casserole. Cover. Microwave at High for 8 to 10 minutes, or until tender, stirring once. Drain. Set aside.

In 1-cup measure, microwave margarine at High for 1¼ to 1½ minutes, or until melted. Add lemon juice. Mix well. Pour margarine mixture over potatoes. Toss to coat. Re-cover. Microwave at High for 2½ to 3 minutes, or until hot.

Per Serving: Calories: 237 • Protein: 4 g. • Carbohydrate: 31 g. • Fat: 12 g. • Cholesterol: 0 • Sodium: 144 mg.
Exchanges: 2 starch, 2 fat

Tricolored Salad

1 medium yellow summer squash, cut in half lengthwise and cubed (¾-inch cubes)
½ medium cucumber, sliced
1 medium tomato, cut into 8 wedges
½ teaspoon onion salt
½ cup ranch dressing

4 servings

Place squash in 1-quart casserole. Cover. Microwave at High for 2 to 2½ minutes, or until tender, stirring once. Drain. Add cucumber, tomato and onion salt. Mix well. Top evenly with dressing.

Per Serving: Calories: 118 • Protein: 1 g. • Carbohydrate: 6 g. • Fat: 10 g. • Cholesterol: 2 mg. • Sodium: 427 mg.
Exchanges: 1 vegetable, 2 fat

Jamaican Flambé

½ cup packed brown sugar
½ cup orange juice
2 tablespoons margarine or butter
3 medium bananas, sliced lengthwise and cut into 1 to 1½-inch lengths
3 tablespoons dark rum
1 pint any flavor sherbet or ice cream

4 servings

In 2-quart casserole, combine sugar, juice and margarine. Microwave at High for 5 to 6 minutes, or until mixture begins to boil, stirring twice. Add bananas and rum. Mix well. Microwave at High for 1½ to 2 minutes, or until bananas are just tender. Cool slightly. Spoon warm sauce over sherbet. Serve immediately.

Per Serving: Calories: 409 • Protein: 2 g. • Carbohydrate: 80 g. • Fat: 8 g. • Cholesterol: 7 mg. • Sodium: 121 mg.
Exchanges: 1 starch, 4½ fruit, 1½ fat

Easy Jambalaya
Mixed Green Salad*
Chocolate Pecan Sandies

Easy Jambalaya

- 2 cups hot water
- 1 pkg. (4.5 oz.) Cajun-style Rice and Sauce Mix
- ½ lb. fully cooked mesquite-smoked sausage, cut into ½-inch slices
- 1 pkg. (10 oz.) frozen peas and carrots
- 1 cup cooked, cubed chicken (about 8 oz.)
- 2 tablespoons catsup

6 servings

In 3-quart casserole, combine water and rice and sauce mix. Cover. Microwave at High for 15 to 20 minutes, or until liquid is absorbed and rice is tender. Add remaining ingredients. Mix well. Re-cover. Microwave at High for 8 to 12 minutes, or until hot, stirring twice.

Per Serving: Calories: 320 • Protein: 22 g.
• Carbohydrate: 24 g. • Fat: 15 g.
• Cholesterol: 55 mg. • Sodium: 1080 mg.
Exchanges: 1 starch, 2 high-fat meat, 1½ vegetable

Chocolate Pecan Sandies

- ½ cup plus 1 tablespoon margarine or butter, divided
- 1¼ cups all-purpose flour
- ¼ cup powdered sugar
- ¼ cup semisweet chocolate chips
- 1 teaspoon shortening
- ⅓ cup dark corn syrup
- 3 tablespoons packed brown sugar
- ½ cup chopped pecans

6 servings
12 tarts

Per Serving: Calories: 450 • Protein: 4 g.
• Carbohydrate: 51 g. • Fat: 27 g. •
Cholesterol: 0 • Sodium: 216 mg.
Exchanges: 2 starch, 1½ fruit, 5 fat

How to Make Chocolate Pecan Sandies

Heat conventional oven to 400°F. In small mixing bowl, microwave ½ cup margarine at 30% (Medium Low) for 15 to 45 seconds, or until margarine is softened, rotating bowl every 15 seconds.

Combine softened margarine, flour and powdered sugar in food processor. Process until soft dough forms. Divide dough into 12 pieces. Press dough into bottoms and ½ inch up sides of muffin pan cups.

Prick bottom of each shell with fork. Bake for 12 to 14 minutes, or until light golden brown. Cool shells in pan for 10 minutes. Carefully remove shells from pan. Set aside.

Combine chocolate chips and shortening in 1-cup measure. Microwave at 50% (Medium) for 2 to 3 minutes, or until chocolate is glossy and can be stirred smooth. Spoon chocolate evenly into each shell. Set shells aside.

Combine corn syrup, brown sugar and remaining 1 tablespoon margarine in 2-cup measure. Microwave at 50% (Medium) for 2½ to 3 minutes, or until mixture thickens and boils slightly, stirring every minute. Stir in pecans. Spoon evenly over chocolate.

Simple Elegance

Raspberry-glazed Turkey Tenderloin Slices   Garlic Green Beans   Dinner Rolls*
White Chocolate Peppermint Mousse, page 152

Garlic Green Beans

2 tablespoons margarine or
   butter
1 clove garlic, minced
¼ teaspoon salt
⅛ teaspoon pepper
2 cups fresh green beans
   (8 oz.)

In 2-quart casserole, microwave margarine at High for 45 seconds to 1 minute, or until melted. Add garlic, salt and pepper. Mix well. Add green beans. Toss to coat. Cover. Microwave at High for 6 to 10 minutes, or until beans are tender-crisp, stirring once.

Per Serving: Calories: 70 • Protein: 1 g. • Carbohydrate: 4 g. • Fat: 6 g. • Cholesterol: 1 mg. • Sodium: 204 mg.
Exchanges: 1 vegetable, 1 fat

4 servings

Raspberry-glazed Turkey Tenderloin Slices

2 turkey tenderloins (6 to 8 oz. each)
   Cayenne
1½ teaspoons cornstarch
⅓ cup raspberry jelly
2 tablespoons rosé wine
1 tablespoon catsup
1 clove garlic, minced
½ teaspoon cream-style horseradish

4 servings

Place tenderloins in 8-inch square baking dish. Sprinkle lightly with cayenne. Cover with plastic wrap. Microwave at 70% (Medium High) for 10 to 16 minutes, or until turkey is firm and no longer pink, rearranging twice.

Slice each tenderloin diagonally into 10 pieces. Arrange 5 pieces on each individual serving plate. Set aside.

Place cornstarch in 2-cup measure. Blend in remaining ingredients. Microwave at High for 1½ to 3 minutes, or until sauce is thickened and translucent, stirring after every minute.

Spoon sauce over tenderloin slices. Garnish with fresh raspberries, if desired.

Per Serving: Calories: 198 • Protein: 26 g. • Carbohydrate: 20 g. • Fat: 1 g. • Cholesterol: 71 mg. • Sodium: 94 mg.
Exchanges: 3 lean meat, 1 fruit

Light & Speedy Supper

Sweet Dilled Chicken   Lightly Seasoned Summer Vegetables
Poached Peach Melba

Sweet Dilled Chicken

Marinade:
½ cup beer
¼ cup vegetable oil
1 tablespoon dried dill weed
1 tablespoon grated Parmesan cheese
2 teaspoons sugar
¼ teaspoon garlic powder

2 boneless whole chicken breasts (8 to 10 oz.
    each), split in half, skin removed

4 servings

In 9-inch round cake dish, combine all marinade ingredients. Add chicken. Cover with plastic wrap. Marinate in refrigerator at least 2 hours. Drain and discard marinade. Re-cover with plastic wrap. Microwave at High for 8 to 10 minutes, or until juices run clear and meat is no longer pink, re-arranging pieces once.

Per Serving: Calories: 178 • Protein: 27 g. • Carbohydrate: 1 g.
• Fat: 7 g. • Cholesterol: 73 mg. • Sodium: 71 mg.
Exchanges: 3 lean meat

Lightly Seasoned Summer Vegetables

1 small eggplant (about 1 lb.), cut into
    2½ × 1-inch strips
2 tablespoons margarine or butter
¼ teaspoon garlic powder
1 medium yellow summer squash, cut into
    2½ × 1-inch strips
1 medium zucchini squash, cut into 2½ × 1-inch
    strips
1 tablespoon red wine vinegar
1 tablespoon grated Parmesan cheese

4 servings

In 2-quart casserole, place eggplant, margarine and garlic powder. Cover. Microwave at High for 6 minutes, stirring once. Add squashes. Re-cover. Microwave at High for 5 to 7 minutes, or until eggplant is translucent and squashes are tender-crisp, stirring once. Sprinkle with vinegar and Parmesan cheese.

Per Serving: Calories: 100 • Protein: 3 g. • Carbohydrate: 10 g.
• Fat: 6 g. • Cholesterol: 1 mg. • Sodium: 102 mg.
Exchanges: 2 vegetable, 1 fat

Poached Peach Melba

1 pkg. (10 oz.) frozen
    raspberries in light syrup
2 cups hot water
1 cup sugar
2 tablespoons lemon juice
1 cinnamon stick
4 fresh peaches, peeled, halved
    and pitted

4 servings

Cut slit in pouch containing raspberries. Place on plate. Microwave at High for 1½ to 3 minutes, or until raspberries are defrosted, rotating plate once. In food processor or blender, process raspberries until smooth. Strain raspberry sauce. Discard seeds. Cover sauce. Chill.

In 2-quart casserole, combine water, sugar, lemon juice and cinnamon stick. Cover. Microwave at High for 8 to 12 minutes, or until water begins to boil. Add peaches. Re-cover. Microwave at High for 5 to 8 minutes, or until peaches are soft, stirring once.

Using slotted spoon, remove peaches from sugar water. Place 2 peach halves on each of 4 dessert plates. Spoon sauce evenly over each dessert. Garnish with fresh mint, if desired.

Per Serving: Calories: 110 • Protein: 1 g. • Carbohydrate: 28 g. • Fat: 0
• Cholesterol: 0 • Sodium: 1 mg.
Exchanges: 2 fruit

Acapulco Evening

Mexican Kabobs   Hot Jicama Salad
Corn Bread Sticks*   Strawberry Margarita Pie, page 147

Mexican Kabobs

¾ lb. boneless beef sirloin or top
    round steak, about 1 inch
    thick, cut into twelve ¼-inch
    strips
¼ cup tequila
2 tablespoons Worcestershire
    sauce

½ teaspoon instant minced
    garlic
6 whole fresh mushrooms
12 cherry tomatoes
3 small onions, quartered
    (12 wedges)
6 wooden skewers (12-inch)
1 lime, cut into 6 wedges

6 servings

In 1-quart casserole, combine beef strips, tequila, Worcestershire sauce and garlic. Mix well. Cover. Marinate in refrigerator 1 to 2 hours. Drain, reserving marinade. Set marinade aside.

Thread meat and vegetables onto skewers, placing mushrooms in center of skewers. Place kabobs on microwave roasting rack. Brush with reserved marinade. Cover with wax paper or microwave cooking paper. Microwave at High for 5 minutes. Rearrange and turn kabobs over. Brush with marinade. Microwave at High for 5 to 7 minutes longer, or until meat is no longer pink. Serve with lime wedges.

Per Serving: Calories: 121 • Protein: 12 g. • Carbohydrate: 5 g. • Fat: 3 g.
• Cholesterol: 33 mg. • Sodium: 83 mg.
Exchanges: 1½ lean meat, 1 vegetable

Hot Jicama Salad

1½ cups julienne jicama
    (2 × ¼-inch strips)
1 cup julienne carrots
    (2 × ¼-inch strips)
1 cup julienne green and red
    pepper (2 × ¼-inch strips)
¼ cup sliced green onions

¼ cup vegetable oil
2 tablespoons fresh lime juice
2 tablespoons water
2 teaspoons sugar
1 tablespoon finely chopped
    fresh cilantro leaves

6 servings

In medium mixing bowl, combine vegetables. Cover with plastic wrap. Microwave at High for 5 to 6 minutes, or until tender-crisp, stirring once. Drain. Set aside.

In small mixing bowl, combine remaining ingredients. Pour over hot salad. Toss to coat. Serve immediately.

Per Serving: Calories: 121 • Protein: 1 g. • Carbohydrate: 10 g. • Fat: 9 g.
• Cholesterol: 0 • Sodium: 8 mg.
Exchanges: ½ starch, ½ vegetable, 1½ fat

Simply Seafood Supper

Seafood Supreme   *Blueberry Orange Wilted Salad*   *Sorbet with Almond Cookies**

Blueberry Orange Wilted Salad

8 cups torn leaf lettuce
1 cup fresh blueberries
2 tablespoons chopped walnuts
2 tablespoons vegetable oil
2 tablespoons water
1 tablespoon frozen orange
   juice concentrate, defrosted
1 tablespoon white vinegar
1 tablespoon honey

6 servings

In large mixing bowl or salad bowl, combine lettuce, blueberries and walnuts. Set aside.

In 1 cup measure, combine remaining ingredients. Microwave at High for 1 to 1½ minutes, or until mixture is hot, stirring twice. Pour over salad mixture. Toss to coat. Serve immediately.

Per Serving: Calories: 98 • Protein: 2 g. • Carbohydrate: 11 g. • Fat: 6 g.
• Cholesterol: 0 • Sodium: 9 mg.
Exchanges: ½ vegetable, ½ fruit, 1 fat

Seafood Supreme

1 pkg. (10 oz.) frozen puff
   pastry shells
¼ cup margarine or butter
⅓ cup all-purpose flour
½ teaspoon salt
¼ teaspoon white pepper
2 cups milk
¼ cup white wine
2 tablespoons grated
   Parmesan cheese
1 pkg. (10 oz.) frozen
   asparagus cuts
1 pkg. (10 oz.) frozen baby
   carrots
1 pkg. (6 oz.) frozen cooked
   deveined medium shrimp,
   defrosted and drained

6 servings

Prepare pastry shells as directed on package. Set aside. In 4-cup measure, microwave margarine at High for 1¼ to 1½ minutes, or until melted. Stir in flour, salt and pepper. Blend in milk and wine. Microwave at High for 7 to 9 minutes, or until mixture thickens and bubbles, stirring 3 times.

Stir in Parmesan cheese, asparagus, carrots and shrimp. Microwave at 70% (Medium High) for 3 to 4 minutes, or until hot. Spoon about ¾ cup mixture into each pastry shell.

Per Serving: Calories: 405 • Protein: 15 g. • Carbohydrate: 33 g. • Fat: 23 g.
• Cholesterol: 63 mg. • Sodium: 665 mg.
Exchanges: 1½ starch, 1 lean meat, 2 vegetable, 4 fat

Lemon Scallops en Papillote

1 pkg. (10 oz.) frozen asparagus spears	2 tablespoons fresh lemon juice
1 cup thinly sliced carrots	Dried dill weed
1 lb. bay scallops	Lemon pepper
¼ cup margarine or butter	

4 servings

Per Serving: Calories: 234 • Protein: 22 g. • Carbohydrate: 10 g. • Fat: 13 g. • Cholesterol: 37 mg. • Sodium: 372 mg.
Exchanges: 3 lean meat, 2 vegetable, 1 fat

How to Microwave Lemon Scallops en Papillote

Place asparagus and carrots in 1½-quart casserole. Cover. Microwave at High for 4 to 6 minutes, or until asparagus is defrosted. Drain. Set aside. Fold four 12 × 12-inch sheets of microwave cooking paper in half. Stack papers on top of each other. Draw half heart shape, starting at fold.

Cut out hearts. On each, arrange one-fourth of vegetable mixture and scallops next to foldline. In small bowl, microwave margarine at High for 1¼ to 1½ minutes, or until melted. Add lemon juice. Mix well. Spoon one-fourth of margarine mixture over scallops and vegetables.

Sprinkle with dill weed and lemon pepper. Refold paper over scallops and vegetables. Starting from one end, fold a short length of paper edges together, then fold again. Continue folding until cut edges are completely sealed. Repeat for remaining packets.

Place two packets on plate, spacing at least 2 inches apart. Microwave at High for 4 to 6 minutes, rearranging packets once. Let stand, unopened, for 3 minutes. Repeat with remaining packets. To serve, place packets on dinner plates. Cut with scissors or tear to open.

Peaches & Blueberries with Almond Custard

2	cups frozen peach slices
1½	cups fresh blueberries
⅓	cup sugar
2	tablespoons cornstarch
1½	cups milk
2	egg yolks
½	teaspoon almond extract

4 servings

Place peaches in 2-quart casserole. Cover. Microwave at High for 2 to 4 minutes, or until defrosted, stirring once. Drain. Add blueberries. Mix well. Spoon fruit evenly into 4 individual serving bowls. Cover with plastic wrap. Chill.

In 4-cup measure, combine sugar and cornstarch. Blend in milk with whisk. Microwave at High for 5 to 7 minutes, or until mixture is thickened and translucent, stirring after first 2 minutes, then after every minute. Stir small amount of hot mixture gradually into egg yolks. Blend yolks back into hot mixture. Microwave at 50% (Medium) for 1 minute. Cool slightly. Stir in almond extract. Serve warm over fruit mixture.

Per Serving: Calories: 223 • Protein: 5 g. • Carbohydrate: 42 g. • Fat: 5 g. • Cholesterol: 143 mg. • Sodium: 53 mg.
Exchanges: 2½ fruit, ½ low-fat milk, ½ fat

Savory Potato & Mushroom Frittata

12 oz. new potatoes, cut into
    ½-inch chunks
2 cups thinly sliced fresh
    mushrooms
2 cloves garlic, minced
½ cup thinly sliced leeks or
    onion
½ cup julienne red pepper
    (2 × ¼-inch strips)
2 tablespoons all-purpose flour
8 eggs, beaten
¼ cup milk
½ teaspoon salt
¼ teaspoon coarsely ground
    black pepper

4 to 6 servings

In 2-quart casserole, combine potatoes, mushrooms and garlic. Cover. Microwave at High for 7 to 10 minutes, or until potatoes are tender, stirring once. Add leeks and red pepper strips. Re-cover. Microwave at High for 1 to 3 minutes, or until vegetables are tender-crisp. Drain. Add flour. Toss to coat. Set aside.

In 8-cup measure, beat together eggs, milk, salt and pepper with whisk. Add vegetable mixture. Mix well. Microwave at High for 3 to 3½ minutes, or until mixture is hot and begins to set around edges, stirring with whisk after each minute. Pour mixture into 10-inch pie plate. Microwave at 70% (Medium High) for 12 to 19 minutes, or until mixture is set, lifting edges several times during cooking. Let stand for 5 minutes.

Per Serving: Calories: 179 • Protein: 11 g. • Carbohydrate: 18 g. • Fat: 7 g.
• Cholesterol: 286 mg. • Sodium: 275 mg.
Exchanges: 1 starch, 1 medium-fat meat, ½ vegetable

Country Herb & Tomato Rolls

1 pkg. (8 oz.) refrigerated
    crescent rolls
¼ cup seeded chopped tomato
1 tablespoon sliced green
    onion
1 tablespoon grated Parmesan
    cheese
½ teaspoon dried basil leaves
⅛ teaspoon garlic powder

8 rolls

Heat conventional oven to 375°F. Remove crescent roll dough from package. Unroll. Press perforations to seal. Sprinkle evenly with remaining ingredients. Roll up dough starting with long side. Slice into 8 rolls.

Place rolls cut-sides-up on ungreased baking sheet. Flatten slightly to 1-inch height. Bake for 10 to 12 minutes, or until deep golden brown. Remove to cooling rack.

Per Serving: Calories: 99 • Protein: 2 g. • Carbohydrate: 13 g. • Fat: 4 g.
• Cholesterol: 1 mg. • Sodium: 348 mg.
Exchanges: 1 starch, ½ fat

Chicken Dijon

⅓ cup unseasoned dry bread
    crumbs
1 tablespoon dried parsley
    flakes
½ teaspoon dried thyme leaves
¼ teaspoon salt
¼ teaspoon cracked pepper
2 tablespoons Dijon mustard
1 tablespoon cream-style
    horseradish
2 bone-in whole chicken
    breasts (10 to 12 oz. each),
    split in half, skin removed

4 servings

In 9-inch pie plate, combine
bread crumbs, parsley flakes,
thyme, salt and pepper. Set aside.
In small bowl, combine mustard
and horseradish. Brush chicken
breasts evenly with Dijon mixture.
Dredge each chicken breast
evenly in crumb mixture, pressing lightly to coat both sides.

Arrange chicken breasts on
roasting rack with meaty portions
toward outside. Cover with wax
paper or microwave cooking
paper. Microwave at High for 10
to 14 minutes, or until meat near
bone is no longer pink and juices
run clear, rearranging twice.

Per Serving: Calories: 220 • Protein: 34 g.
• Carbohydrate: 7 g. • Fat: 5 g. •
Cholesterol: 91 mg. • Sodium: 499 mg.
Exchanges: ½ starch, 4 lean meat

Sweet Carrot, Cauliflower & Spinach

2 tablespoons margarine or
    butter
¼ cup packed brown sugar
½ teaspoon dry mustard
¼ teaspoon salt
2 cups sliced fresh
    cauliflowerets
1 cup diagonally sliced carrots
    (⅛-inch slices)
2 cups torn fresh spinach
    leaves

4 servings

In 2-quart casserole, microwave
margarine at High for 45 seconds
to 1 minute, or until melted. Add
brown sugar, dry mustard and
salt. Mix well.

Add cauliflowerets and carrots.
Toss to coat. Cover. Microwave
at High for 4 to 7 minutes, or until
vegetables are tender-crisp. Add
spinach. Toss to coat.

Per Serving: Calories: 134 • Protein: 2 g.
• Carbohydrate: 20 g. • Fat: 6 g. •
Cholesterol: 0 • Sodium: 245 mg.
Exchanges: 4 vegetable, 1 fat

Crunchy Coffee Ice Cream Torte

¼ cup water
2 tablespoons instant coffee
    crystals
2 pints vanilla ice cream
20 coarsely chopped chocolate
    sandwich cookies

10 servings

In 1-cup measure, microwave
water at High for 1 to 1½ minutes,
or until it begins to boil. Add coffee crystals. Mix well. Set aside.

Remove lid from each pint of ice
cream. Using scissors, cut down
sides of each carton to remove
ice cream.

Place ice cream in medium
mixing bowl. Microwave at 30%
(Medium Low) for 1½ to 3 minutes, or until ice cream can be
stirred smooth, stirring twice.
Add coffee and cookie crumbs.
Mix well. Spoon evenly into 8-inch
springform pan. Freeze about 4
hours, or until firm. Garnish with
whipped topping and maraschino
cherries, if desired.

Per Serving: Calories: 208 • Protein: 3 g.
• Carbohydrate: 27 g. • Fat: 10 g. •
Cholesterol: 32 mg. • Sodium: 143 mg.
Exchanges: 1½ starch, 2 fat

Fast Finishes

Chocolate, Fruit & Cheese Pie

Peanut Butter Cream Pie

1 pkg. (8 oz.) cream cheese
½ cup powdered sugar
½ cup milk
½ cup creamy peanut butter
1½ cups prepared whipped
     topping
1 graham cracker crust
     (8-inch)
3 tablespoons semisweet
     chocolate chips
½ teaspoon vegetable oil

8 servings

In medium mixing bowl, microwave cream cheese at 50% (Medium) for 1½ to 3 minutes, or until softened, stirring once. Add sugar, milk and peanut butter. Beat at medium speed of electric mixer until smooth. Fold in whipped topping. Spoon filling evenly into crust. Set aside.

In small bowl, combine chocolate chips and oil. Microwave at High for 1 to 1½ minutes, or until chocolate is glossy and mixture can be stirred smooth, stirring once. Drizzle chocolate in horizontal lines over filling. Marble by pulling knife vertically through chocolate lines. Chill 2 hours, or until firm.

Per Serving: Calories: 430 • Protein: 9 g. • Carbohydrate: 34 g. • Fat: 31 g. • Cholesterol: 34 mg. • Sodium: 375 mg.

Exchanges: 1 starch, 1 fruit, ½ low-fat milk, 5 fat

Cherry Peach Cream Pie

  8 oz. cream cheese
¼ cup powdered sugar
  1 tablespoon milk
¼ teaspoon almond extract
  1 graham cracker crust (8-inch)
  2 cups frozen unsweetened
      peach slices
  1 can (21 oz.) cherry pie filling

8 servings

In small mixing bowl, microwave cream cheese at 50% (Medium) for 1½ to 3 minutes, or until softened. Add sugar, milk and extract. Mix well. Spread evenly over crust. Set aside.

Place peaches in 2-quart casserole. Cover. Microwave at High for 2 to 4 minutes, or until defrosted, stirring once. Drain. Add cherry pie filling. Mix well. Spoon pie filling evenly over cream cheese layer. Chill 2 hours, or until firm.

Per Serving: Calories: 504 • Protein: 4 g. • Carbohydrate: 82 g.
• Fat: 19 g. • Cholesterol: 31 mg. • Sodium: 300 mg.
Exchanges: 1 starch, 4½ fruit, 3½ fat

Macaroon Clouds

1 pkg. (8 oz.) cream cheese
⅓ cup powdered sugar
1 tablespoon milk
¼ teaspoon almond extract
1 cup prepared whipped
   topping
¾ cup multicolored miniature
   marshmallows
¾ cup chopped macaroon
   cookies
6 scoops rainbow sherbet

6 servings

Line baking sheet with wax paper or microwave cooking paper.
Set aside.

In 1½-quart casserole, microwave cream cheese at 50% (Medium)
for 1½ to 3 minutes, or until softened. Add sugar, milk and extract.
Beat at medium speed of electric mixer until smooth. Fold in whipped
topping. Add marshmallows and cookies. Mix well.

Spoon mixture into 3-inch circles on prepared baking sheet. Using
back of spoon, form well in center of each circle. Freeze 1 hour, or
until firm. Place macaroon clouds on individual serving plates. Place
1 scoop of sherbet in center of each.

Per Serving: Calories: 398 • Protein: 5 g. • Carbohydrate: 51 g. • Fat: 21 g.
• Cholesterol: 60 mg. • Sodium: 166 mg.
Exchanges: 2 starch, 1½ fruit, 4 fat

Strawberry Margarita Pie ▶

Nonstick vegetable cooking
   spray
¼ cup plus 1 tablespoon
   margarine or butter
1⅓ cups crushed pretzels
   (about 3½ cups mini
   pretzel twists)
2 tablespoons sugar
2 cups frozen unsweetened
   strawberries
3 cups frozen strawberry-
   banana yogurt
½ can (10 oz.) frozen
   strawberry-flavored
   daiquiri mix
¼ cup tequila or Triple Sec
   (optional)

8 servings

Spray 9-inch pie plate with nonstick vegetable cooking spray.
Set aside.

In medium mixing bowl, microwave margarine at High for 1¼ to
1½ minutes, or until melted. Add
pretzels and sugar. Toss to coat.
Press mixture firmly and evenly
against bottom and sides of prepared pie plate. Microwave at
High for 1½ to 2 minutes, or until
crust is set, rotating once. Cool.

Place strawberries in 1-quart
casserole. Cover. Microwave at
High for 1½ to 2 minutes, or until
partially defrosted. Place strawberries and remaining ingredients in
food processor or blender. Process until smooth.

Spoon filling into cooled crust.
Cover with foil. Freeze about 4
hours, or until firm. Let stand at
room temperature for 20 minutes
before serving.

Per Serving: Calories: 261 • Protein: 3 g.
• Carbohydrate: 40 g. • Fat: 11 g.
• Cholesterol: 4 mg. • Sodium: 285 mg.
Exchanges: ½ starch, 1½ fruit, ½ low-fat
milk, 1½ fat

Chocolate, Fruit & Cheese Pie

1 pkg. (8 oz.) cream cheese
⅓ cup powdered sugar
1 tablespoon milk
1 carton (8 oz.) prepared
   whipped topping
1 chocolate crumb crust
   (8-inch)

1 to 2 cups fresh fruit
   (raspberries, blueberries,
   grapes, sliced kiwifruit,
   strawberries, nectarines)
2 tablespoons semisweet
   chocolate chips
½ teaspoon vegetable oil

6 servings

In 1½-quart casserole, microwave cream cheese at 50% (Medium) for
1½ to 3 minutes, or until softened, stirring once. Add sugar and milk.
Beat at medium speed of electric mixer until smooth. Fold in whipped
topping. Spoon filling into prepared crust. Arrange fruit evenly over
cream cheese layer.

In small bowl, place chocolate chips and oil. Microwave at High for 1
to 1½ minutes, or until chocolate is glossy and mixture can be stirred
smooth. Drizzle chocolate over fruit. Chill 2 hours, or until firm.

Per Serving: Calories: 427 • Protein: 6 g. • Carbohydrate: 34 g. • Fat: 31 g.
• Cholesterol: 54 mg. • Sodium: 257 mg.
Exchanges: 1 starch, 1 fruit, ½ low-fat milk, 5½ fat

Frozen Pumpkin-Ginger Torte

- 1 pkg. (8 oz.) cream cheese
- 1 can (15 oz.) pumpkin
- ½ cup packed brown sugar
- 2 teaspoons pumpkin pie spice
- 2 cups prepared whipped topping
- 6 to 8 gingersnap cookies (2-inch)
- 2 tablespoons finely chopped pecans
- 2 tablespoons margarine or butter

12 servings

In medium mixing bowl, microwave cream cheese at 50% (Medium) for 1½ to 3 minutes, or until softened. Add pumpkin, sugar and pumpkin pie spice. Beat at medium speed of electric mixer until mixture is smooth and creamy. Fold in whipped topping. Spoon into 8-inch springform pan. Set aside.

In food processor or blender, process cookies until crumbly. Add pecans. Set aside. In small mixing bowl, microwave margarine at High for 45 seconds to 1 minute, or until melted. Add cookie crumb mixture. Stir until crumbly. Sprinkle evenly over pumpkin mixture.

Freeze at least 8 hours or overnight. Let stand at room temperature for 20 minutes before cutting.

Per Serving: Calories: 193 • Protein: 2 g. • Carbohydrate: 18 g. • Fat: 13 g. • Cholesterol: 22 mg. • Sodium: 151 mg.
Exchanges: 1 starch, 2½ fat

Peanut Date Bars ▲

- ½ cup margarine or butter
- ¾ cup packed brown sugar
- 1 pkg. (8 oz.) chopped pitted dates
- 1 egg, beaten
- 1 teaspoon vanilla
- 2 cups crisp rice cereal
- 1 cup chopped salted peanuts

24 bars

Grease 11 × 7-inch baking dish. Set aside. In 8-cup measure, microwave margarine at High for 1½ to 1¾ minutes, or until melted. Add sugar and dates. Mix well. Stir in egg and vanilla.

Microwave at 50% (Medium) for 8 to 11 minutes, or until mixture thickens and bubbles, stirring twice. Stir in cereal and peanuts. Mix well. Spread mixture evenly in pan. Cool. Cut into squares.

Per Serving: Calories: 134 • Protein: 2 g. • Carbohydrate: 17 g. • Fat: 7 g. • Cholesterol: 9 mg. • Sodium: 97 mg.
Exchanges: ½ starch, ½ fruit, 1½ fat

Toffee Bar Pie

- 4 chocolate-covered toffee bars (1.2 oz. each)
- 1 cup chopped pecans
- 1½ cups semisweet chocolate chips
- 2 pints butter pecan ice cream

8 servings

Line 9-inch glass pie plate with foil, leaving 2-inch overhang around edges. Set aside. In food processor or blender, process toffee bars and pecans until finely chopped. Set aside.

In 2-cup measure, microwave chocolate chips at 50% (Medium) for 4 to 5 minutes, or until chocolate is glossy and can be stirred smooth, stirring twice.

Add ⅓ cup toffee bar mixture to melted chocolate.

Spread chocolate mixture in even layer over bottom and sides of lined pie plate. Freeze 10 to 15 minutes, or until firm. Remove from freezer.

Remove foil from pie shell. Return pie shell to pie plate.

Remove covers from ice cream. Microwave each pint at 50% (Medium) for 30 seconds to 1 minute, or until softened. Spread 1 pint ice cream into pie shell. Sprinkle with ⅓ cup toffee mixture. Spread remaining 1 pint ice cream over toffee mixture. Sprinkle with remaining ⅓ cup toffee mixture. Freeze at least 8 hours or overnight. Let stand at room temperature for 10 minutes before cutting.

Per Serving: Calories: 506 • Protein: 5 g. • Carbohydrate: 43 g. • Fat: 38 g. • Cholesterol: 30 mg. • Sodium: 105 mg. Exchanges: 2 starch, 1 fruit, 6½ fat

Tropical Coconut Sauce ▲

½ cup shredded coconut
1½ cups half-and-half
½ cup cream of coconut
2 tablespoons cornstarch
¼ teaspoon rum extract

2 cups sauce
16 servings

Spread coconut in even layer in 9-inch pie plate. Microwave at 70% (Medium High) for 3 to 5 minutes, or until light brown, tossing with fork after each minute. Cool.

In 4-cup measure, combine half-and-half, cream of coconut and cornstarch. Beat well with whisk. Microwave at High for 4 to 6 minutes, or until mixture thickens and bubbles, stirring twice. Beat in rum extract. Serve over fresh fruit or ice cream. Sprinkle with toasted coconut.

Per Serving: Calories: 59 • Protein: 1 g. • Carbohydrate: 4 g. • Fat: 5 g. • Cholesterol: 8 mg. • Sodium: 13 mg.
Exchanges: ½ vegetable, 1 fat

Bananas & Oranges with Rum Chocolate Sauce

4 medium bananas, sliced
4 medium oranges, peeled and sectioned
1 teaspoon lemon juice
½ cup semisweet chocolate chips
¼ cup half-and-half
2 teaspoons light rum

4 servings

In medium mixing bowl, combine bananas, oranges and lemon juice. Toss to coat. Set aside.

In 2-cup measure, combine chocolate chips and half-and-half. Microwave at 50% (Medium) for 1½ to 3 minutes, or until mixture can be stirred smooth, stirring once. Add rum. Mix well.

Spoon fruit evenly into 4 individual bowls. Drizzle 2 tablespoons of sauce over each serving.

Per Serving: Calories: 304 • Protein: 4 g. • Carbohydrate: 56 g. • Fat: 10 g. • Cholesterol: 6 mg. • Sodium: 8 mg.
Exchanges: 3½ fruit, 2 fat

Pudding with Cinnamon Pastry & Raspberries

- 1 pkg. (3¼ oz.) chocolate pudding and pie filling
- ¾ teaspoon ground cinnamon, divided
- 2¼ cups milk
- ½ teaspoon almond extract
- 1 pkg. (15 oz.) refrigerated prepared pie crusts
- 2 teaspoons sugar
- 1 tablespoon raspberry jelly
- ½ cup fresh raspberries

6 servings

In 8-cup measure, combine pudding mix, ½ teaspoon cinnamon, the milk and extract. Beat well with whisk. Microwave at High for 6 to 8 minutes, or until mixture thickens and bubbles, stirring twice. Place plastic wrap directly on surface of pudding. Set aside. Continue as directed below.

Per Serving: Calories: 449 • Protein: 8 g. • Carbohydrate: 52 g. • Fat: 24 g. • Cholesterol: 7 mg. • Sodium: 517 mg. Exchanges: 3 starch, ½ fruit, 4 fat

How to Microwave Pudding with Cinnamon Pastry & Raspberries

Microwave one crust pouch at 30% (Medium Low) for 15 to 45 seconds, or until softened. Unfold pastry and remove top piece of plastic wrap. Cut twelve 2 to 3-inch shapes. Combine sugar and remaining ¼ teaspoon cinnamon in small bowl.

Sprinkle evenly over pastry. Place pastry on wax paper or microwave cooking paper. Microwave at High for 4 to 6 minutes, or until dry and firm and golden spots begin to appear. Remove from wax paper. Set aside.

Place jelly in small bowl. Microwave at High for 15 to 45 seconds, or until melted. Spoon warm pudding evenly onto 6 dessert plates. Arrange 2 pastry shapes over pudding on each plate. Drizzle evenly with jelly. Garnish with raspberries.

White Chocolate Peppermint Mousse ◄

1 pkg. (3⅛ oz.) vanilla pudding
   and pie filling
2 cups milk
½ teaspoon peppermint extract
2 white baking bars
   (2 oz. each)
1 carton (12 oz.) prepared
   whipped topping

6 servings

Place pudding mix in 8-cup measure. Blend in milk and extract. Microwave at High for 6 to 9 minutes, or until mixture thickens and bubbles, stirring after first 3 minutes and then every minute. Place plastic wrap directly on surface of pudding. Chill about 4 hours, or until completely cool.

In small mixing bowl, microwave baking bars at 50% (Medium) for 3 to 4 minutes, or until bars are glossy and can be stirred smooth, stirring once. Add to chilled pudding. Mix well. Fold in whipped topping.

Spoon mousse into parfait glasses. Sprinkle with crushed peppermint candies, if desired.

Per Serving: Calories: 303 • Protein: 6 g.
• Carbohydrate: 38 g. • Fat: 15 g. •
Cholesterol: 15 mg. • Sodium: 161 mg.
Exchanges: 2 starch, ½ low-fat milk, 2½ fat

Sherry Marmalade Oranges

2 large oranges, peeled,
   cut into ¼-inch slices
¼ cup orange marmalade

1 tablespoon dry sherry
2 tablespoons chopped
   pecans

4 servings

In 9-inch pie plate, arrange orange slices in overlapping circle. In small bowl, combine marmalade and sherry. Spoon over oranges; top with pecans. Cover with wax paper or microwave cooking paper. Microwave at High for 3 to 4 minutes, or until glazed and hot, rotating once.

Per Serving: Calories: 121 • Protein: 1 g. • Carbohydrate: 25 g. • Fat: 3 g.
• Cholesterol: 0 • Sodium: 3 mg.
Exchanges: 1½ fruit, ½ fat

Orange Caramel Pears ▲

½ cup caramel topping
1 tablespoon frozen orange
   juice concentrate
⅓ cup finely chopped pecans
2 medium fresh pears, cored
   and sliced

4 servings

In 4-cup measure, combine caramel topping and orange juice concentrate. Microwave at High for 1 to 1½ minutes, or until hot, stirring once. Add pecans. Mix well. Arrange pear slices on 4 individual dessert plates. Spoon warm caramel mixture over pears.

Per Serving: Calories: 209 • Protein: 1 g.
• Carbohydrate: 47 g. • Fat: 3 g. •
Cholesterol: 9 mg. • Sodium: 35 mg.
Exchanges: 3 fruit, ½ fat

Pecan Apple Crumble

5 pecan shortbread cookies
   (2 to 2¼-inch)
¼ teaspoon ground cinnamon
⅛ teaspoon ground cloves

1 can (20 oz.) apple pie filling
¼ cup raisins
2 tablespoons margarine or
   butter

4 servings

In food processor or blender, process cookies, cinnamon and cloves until crumbly. Set aside.

Divide apple pie filling evenly among four 10-ounce custard cups. Add 1 tablespoon raisins to each custard cup. Stir to combine. Sprinkle each evenly with cookie crumb mixture.

In small bowl, microwave margarine at High for 45 seconds to 1 minute, or until melted. Drizzle evenly over crumb mixture.

Arrange custard cups in microwave. Microwave at High for 6 to 8 minutes, or until mixture begins to bubble around edges, rearranging custard cups once. Cool 5 to 10 minutes. Serve warm. Top with ice cream, if desired.

Per Serving: Calories: 388 • Protein: 1 g. • Carbohydrate: 83 g. • Fat: 8 g.
• Cholesterol: 4 mg. • Sodium: 114 mg.
Exchanges: 1 starch, 4½ fruit, 1 fat

Index